Money Matters for TEENS

WORKBOOK

Age 11–14 Edition

Money Matters for

WORKBOOK
Age 11–14 Edition

Written by
Larry Burkett
with **Todd Temple**

Illustrated by Chris Kielesinski

MOODY PRESS
CHICAGO

© 1998 by Larry Burkett
Illustrations © 1998 by Lauree and L. Allen Burkett

Project Coordinator: *L. Allen Burkett*
Editor: *Adeline Griffith*

For Lightwave
Project Editor: *K. Christie Bowler*
Art Director: *Terry Van Roon*
Illustrator: *Chris Kielesinski*
Inker: *Ken Save*

Adapted and rewritten from *Surviving the Money Jungle.*

All Scripture quotations, unless indicated, are taken from the *Holy Bible: New International Version*®. NIV © 1973, 1978, 1984 by International Bible Society. Used by permission of Zondervan Publishing House. All rights reserved.

The "NIV" and "New International Version" trademarks are registered in the United States Patent and Trademark Office by International Bible Society. Use of either trademark requires permission of International Bible Society.

ISBN: 0-8024-6345-2

Printed in the United States of America

Contents

Introduction 7

Chapter 1
Money Basics 9

Chapter 2
How Banks Work 17

Chapter 3
The Checkbook 27

Chapter 4
Reconciling a Checking Account 37

Chapter 5
Keeping Track of All That Money 45

Chapter 6
Managing Bigger Budgets 53

Chapter 7
Giving It Back 61

Chapter 8
How To Make Money with Money 69

Chapter 9
How To Spend Money Wisely 77

Chapter 10
How Loans Work 85

Chapter 11
How To Borrow Money 93

Chapter 12
How To Change the World with Your Money 99

Forms 106

Introduction

Money is merely a convenient means of exchanging goods and services without having to carry the goods around with you. Anything can be used as money: Seashells were used as money in Hawaii at one time; tulip bulbs were used as money in Holland; iron was used as money among Native American tribes; and paper is used as money today.

The paper money we use today wears out easily and thus has to be replaced; plus, since there's a lot of paper available, it's pretty easy to counterfeit. But, since our government vigorously prosecutes counterfeiters, people still trust our paper money.

Money is neither good nor bad, in and of itself, but it can be used for good or bad. Money invested in cancer research is good, but money used to buy illegal drugs is bad.

Money used to buy food and housing for a family is good, but if that same family buys too much junk food and a house that is too expensive for their income it can be bad. So it's not money or credit that's bad; it's the *misuse* of money and credit that's bad.

Credit, when used properly in a business, helps to create jobs. Credit, when used to take an expensive vacation, can lead to debt and depression.

The purpose of this workbook is to help you understand how to use money properly and make intelligent decisions based on what God's Word says and not what some television ad says.

We live in a very complicated world today, and it's going to get even more complicated. In my generation, our financial choices were a whole lot simpler. Basically, as teenagers we had to decide what to buy with the money we had. There were no credit cards or student loans, and when we bought something on time we used the layaway plan (the merchant kept the goods until we paid them off).

You have a great opportunity to learn at a young age what takes most people 40 or more years to learn: how to make good financial decisions. In this study, you'll learn how to balance a checkbook, handle a credit card, buy a car, even how to choose the right insurance. Once you know all this, you can help your parents do it too (just kidding)!

The lessons you learn here will last the rest of your life. You'll be prepared to face the world armed with ways of doing things that are based on the Bible. God wants each of us to become good stewards (managers of His property). Once you are a good steward, God can entrust greater things to you.

The "how-to"s are found in this workbook, and the "why-to"s are found in the companion trade book, *Money Matters for Teens*, produced by my son and daughter-in-law, Allen and Lauree Burkett, published by Moody Press. Allen and

Lauree founded *Money Matters for Teens*™ and *Money Matters for Kids*™ to help young people understand and put into practice the principles of stewardship. Look for their logo (as it appears on this workbook) on other titles created with you in mind.

The lessons you learn here will last the rest of your life. I promise that the time you spend on this study will pay great dividends for the rest of your life.

God bless you!
Larry Burkett

CHAPTER 1
Money Basics

Chapter 1

Money Basics

The average American teenager spends nearly $3,000 a year. Does that number seem too high to you? Add all the money you get from your parents or grandparents, plus any money you make from doing chores or part-time jobs. And don't forget those gifts of money you get for birthdays or Christmas! Your total may be less than $3,000, but it still adds up to a decent stack of cash. Let's look at where your money went—and why.

Learning About Money

Money is one of the world's most popular inventions. Just about everyone enjoys having money. We like to have money. And we like to *spend* money!

But *learning* about money is a different thing. As a study subject, most people would put it near the bottom of their things-I'd-most-like-to-know list. They hear words like *budget, accounting, interest,* and *loans* and say, "Get out of here! I'm not interested in that stuff."

This is especially true with teenagers. Many students feel it's not important right now because they have so little money to worry about. Is that true for you? Maybe you're saying to yourself, "Sure, I'll learn about money . . . as soon as I *have* some!" Well, guess what? You may not have much, but you have enough to matter—at least in the eyes of the people who sell products to young people.

American teenagers spend over $90 *billion* each year! What's more, everyone from Nike® to Nintendo® knows this fact; and they want their share. The people who sell music (cassettes, CDs), movies, munchies, makeup, milk shakes, and Macintoshes have your number. And they are running it through their calculators: "How much money can we get teenagers to spend on *our* products?"

If you don't take control of your money, someone else will.

That's reason enough why you should learn how to manage your money. People marketing products to youth are spending billions in advertising, employing an army of marketing experts, and inventing powerful and creative ways to separate you from your money.

Of course, some of what they sell is stuff you need. And much of it is what makes your life more enjoyable. But wouldn't you like to have *more* money to buy the things that are important to you? You can if you will take these suggestions.

That's what this book is all about. We'll show you how to take control of your money so you can do these things. You'll learn skills that will help you right now *and* also prepare you for a successful financial future. These skills work on *any* amount of money—a $5 allowance or a $5,000 paycheck. No matter how much money you have, you can manage it with the right skills.

- Pay fair price for quality items.
- Avoid being ripped off by misleading ads and salespeople.
- Stay out of debt.
- Save for a car, college, your own business.
- Give money away to make a difference in the world.
- Save money to buy the things you want and do things with your friends.

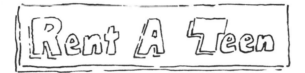

GARDENER

TEETH FLOSSING

CARPENTRY

Count Your Money

How much money passes through your hands in a year? In the spaces below, write down how much money you get on average in a year. If you can't remember what you got the previous year, calculate it on one month and multiply by twelve. You'll be surprised!

Allowance: If you receive allowance weekly, multiply it by 52.　TOTAL _____

Odd jobs: If you have/had a variety of odd jobs, you might want to list them separately. For example: newspaper route, babysitting, mowing lawns.

1. _____　　4. _____

2. _____　　5. _____

3. _____　　6. _____　TOTAL _____

Extra money from parents: This might include money you borrowed while you were out shopping (don't forget to repay it) or just extra gifts of money for specific needs, outings, and so on. We've suggested some categories and left blanks for others.

1. Lunch money _____　　4. Gift _____

2. Outings _____　　5. _____

3. Achievement reward _____　　6. _____　TOTAL _____

Birthday: _____　_____　TOTAL _____

Christmas: _____　_____　TOTAL _____

Gifts from others besides your parents: aunts and uncles, family friends:

1. _____　　3. _____

2. _____　　4. _____　TOTAL _____

Other money you received from places other than those mentioned above:

1. _____　　3. _____

2. _____　　4. _____　TOTAL _____

Now add up the totals from all the sections.　　**YEAR TOTAL** _____

How To Buy Money

Before we talk about how to manage money, you need to understand where money comes from. As our parents have told us (about 3,000 times), "Money doesn't grow on trees."

Simply put, you *buy* money. You can purchase money with all sorts of things.

You can buy money with products. If you're a farmer, you pay in pigs, peaches, or potatoes. If you own real estate, you can offer acres of land, apartments, or office buildings. Just about any *thing* can be used to purchase money. That is, if somebody *wants* what you have and has enough money.

Most of us buy our money with our time and talents. Talents come in different denominations: You can buy $5 in one hour if you know how to sew on fabric (a dress or a suit). You can buy $5,000 in an hour if you can sew up a person after putting in a new heart. Money can be made as long as someone is willing to "trade" with you.

Of course, time doesn't grow on trees, either. Every hour you sell for money is no longer available for other investments—friendships, family, God, education, fun, and sleep. How much time you sell depends on how much these other priorities are worth to you.

Putting a Price Tag on Money

Some people pay a very high price for money. They sacrifice their families, their friendships, their faith. In other words, they "pay the price" with these things. (So *that's* where the expression came from!)

> *Where your treasure is, there your heart will be also.*
> — *Jesus*

What's money worth to you? You set the price. You need a certain amount of money to support other priorities. (Your dad or mom sells time *away* from the family so he or she can afford to buy time *with* the family—a family that's fed and clothed and under a roof.)

If saving money for your future, or giving to your church, or helping the needy, or going on a trip with your youth group is important to you, you'll have to sell some time to do it. In a way, time *is* money.

> *Good money management gives you more money and more time for what's important to you.*

That's why you must take control of your money. If you waste money through making the wrong choices and bad management, you have less money for your priorities. Then you have to spend more time *working* to buy more money—time away from your priorities.

All of this money management stuff is especially important for Christians. The Bible tells us that God is the owner of everything in this world. That includes you, your time, and your money. You don't really *own* anything! You're just managing these things for God.

God wants you to make wise investments with *His* time and money. He has great plans for you, and He wants you to use this time and money to make a difference in the lives of the people around you. If you waste His resources, you can't do all the great things He's got planned for you. If you manage wisely, He'll use you to change the world!

The lessons in this book will help you take the control of this time and money away from lenders, advertisers, and stores and put it where it belongs: with you and God.

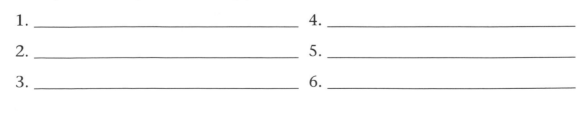
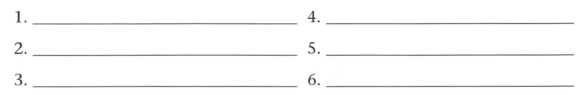

Where Did All Your Money Go?

Are you surprised at the large amount of money that passes through your hands each year? Think about the possibilities. If you had a spending plan, what could you have done with all that money you would have saved? Make a list.

1. _____   4. _____

2. _____   5. _____

3. _____   6. _____

Now look at what you did with all that money. What of lasting value (including experiences) do you have to show for that year's worth of money?

1. _____   4. _____

2. _____   5. _____

3. _____   6. _____

Compare your lists. Which one is more satisfactory? What will you do with your money this coming year?

1. _____   4. _____

2. _____   5. _____

3. _____   6. _____

Rewind

1. American teenagers spend over $90 billion a year. Youth marketers know that—they want their share.

2. Good money management takes the control of your money out of youth marketers' hands.

3. Most people get money by selling their time.

4. You set the price on money: What you are willing to pay for it depends on your priorities.

5. Good money management gives you more money and more time for what's important in life.

notes

_____

_____

_____

_____

_____

_____

_____

_____

_____

_____

_____

_____

_____

_____

notes

CHAPTER
2
How Banks Work

Chapter 2

How Banks Work

Nearly everyone in the country has some kind of bank account. Amazingly, most people don't know much about how banks work. You're about to learn what banks do with money: where it goes, how they figure interest, and how they can help people save more money. By the end of this chapter, you'll know more about banking than most adults. Let's step into the vault.

The Money Store

You probably live pretty close to a grocery store. Grocers provide an important service in your community. They buy food products from farmers, dairies, food companies, and other *suppliers;* then they sell these items to *customers.*

Your neighborhood bank does the same thing, except that they don't sell food; they sell *money.* The bank "buys" money from *suppliers*—you and everyone else with a savings account—and *pays* interest for the money (what they pay to use *your* money). Then the bank "sells" the money to *customers*—businesses and individuals who take out loans—and charges *interest* for the money (what you pay to use *their* money).

The grocers buy the products *wholesale* and sell them *retail.* The bankers "buy" the money at *lower interest* and "sell" it at *higher interest.* Of course, you don't hear bankers talking about buying and selling. They call it *borrowing* and *lending.*

GROCERY STORE	LOCAL BANK
buys from suppliers at wholesale prices	*borrows* from depositors at lower interest rates
sells to customers at retail prices	*lends* to borrowers at higher interest rates

Money Jugglers

Many people think that when they deposit money in a savings account, the bank simply stores the cash in the vault, where it gathers dust until they want it back. It doesn't work that way. Banks aren't money *warehouses*—they are money *stores.* They put that money to work by lending it to other people and charging them interest on the loan.

Here's how it works: Let's say that you and nine of your friends have each scraped together $1,000. Congratulations! You all march down to the bank and invest your money in savings accounts that pay 5 percent interest. The bank loves you! That's because the bank can now take each of your $1,000 deposits and lend a full $10,000 to someone else, who will have to pay 10 percent interest. They can afford to pay interest to you (and the other nine) and still make a profit.

But what happens on the day you and your friends decide to withdraw your $1,000 deposits? The bank can't ask the borrower who has your money to return it. They don't have to. On the day of your big withdrawal, the bank has plenty of cash because many other customers have made deposits. They also have a mailbox full of loan payments from people who have borrowed from them. And, just in case, they also keep enough "spare change" in their vault to cover many withdrawals.

Banks are constantly juggling money. If they need more money to lend to people, they may offer a better interest rate on their savings accounts. This will attract more people to open accounts and deposit their money at the bank. Then the bank lends this new money to new borrowers and charges them enough in interest to cover the interest they're paying on their savings accounts.

Your Savings Account

Now that you've seen the big picture, let's look at it in detail. How does the bank take care of *your* savings account? When you deposit your money in a savings account, the bank pays you a fee for letting them use it. As we learned earlier, the fee is called *interest.* The interest is based on a percentage of your *balance* (the amount in your account).

Let's say that the bank pays 12 percent interest on your savings account. (That's much higher than you are likely to get in a *real* bank, but let's use it for illustration.) On official documents and advertisements, the bank will print "12 percent APR." The APR stands for Annual Percentage Rate, which is their way of saying that the interest is figured over one year. If you deposit $100 in your account, you should receive $12 in interest at the end of one year, right? Wrong! Here's why.

Simple Interest

Compound Interest

There are basically two types of interest: *simple* interest and *compound* interest. Simple interest is figured only on the *principal*—your investment. In the first month example, the $100 is your principal. The $12 would be the simple interest you earn on your principal. It's that simple.

But banks don't pay simple interest on savings—and that's a good thing for you. (Banks do sometimes *charge* simple interest on loans. For more on simple interest, see Chapter 10, How Loans Work.)

Banks pay the second type of interest: *compound interest*. Here's the difference: At the end of the first month, the bank pays you the share of the interest that you've earned on your principal *so far*. They can't pay you 12 percent—that's an *annual* rate. So they pay you one month's worth—*one-twelfth* of 12 percent. Of course, that's 1 percent. One percent of $100 is $1. Now you have $101 in your account—that's $100 in principal *and* $1 in interest.

At the end of the second month they do the same thing. They pay you 1 percent interest on the *entire* balance in your account—principal *and* interest.

Here's the important part. Every month, the bank calculates the interest you've earned on the *entire* balance: principal and all the interest you've earned so far. In other words, the bank is paying interest on the interest. And that's what's called *compound interest*.

First Month	
starting balance:	$100.00
monthly interest rate:	x .01
interest:	= $1.00
starting balance:	+ 100.00
new balance:	= $101.00

Second Month	
starting balance:	$101.00
monthly interest rate:	x .01
interest:	= $1.01
starting balance:	+ 101.00
new balance:	= $102.01

By the way, there's no rule that says a bank must compound the interest *monthly*. Some accounts pay interest *daily*. This means they divide the annual interest rate by 365 (instead of 12) and multiply that day's balance by this tiny interest rate. All those smaller interest payments add up to more money for you.

The Yield

We've gone ahead and calculated the monthly, compounding interest on the above deposit for the rest of the year. At the end of 12 months, the balance is $112.68. You've earned $12.68 in interest. But wait. If the bank *pays* 12 percent interest, why do you *receive* 12.68 percent?

That's the beauty of compound interest on a savings account. The interest *on the interest* adds up to more than the annual percentage rate. The 12.68 percent you actually received is called the *yield*. It's a word that farmers use to describe how much crop a particular acre of land produces in one season. In banking, it's used to describe how much money a particular investment *produces* in one year.

When you're shopping around for a savings account to invest in, compare the yields (banks publish the yield next to the percentage rate). An account that yields 5.25 percent pays $5.25 in interest on a $100 investment for one year. A 6.5 percent yield pays $6.50 in interest on the same investment for the same period. It's pretty simple to compare that way.

Keeping Track

One of the purposes of this book is to show you how to manage money wisely. That means keeping track of your money: what you earn, spend, give, and save. Let's work on that last one for a bit: tracking what you save.

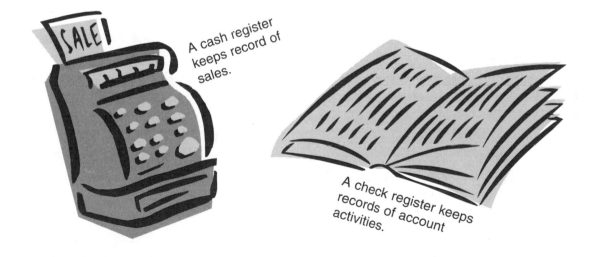

A cash register keeps record of sales.

A check register keeps records of account activities.

When you open a savings account, your bank may give you a *savings account register*. This little booklet contains columns and boxes that make it easy to record your deposits, withdrawals, and interest payments. We've reprinted a page from a savings account register that you can use to record some imaginary transactions.

Step 1: Make and Record Your Transactions

Let's say that you open a savings account on March 1 and deposit $50. A week later you deposit $10; the next week, $20. And during the last week of the month, you put in another $5. Each time you make a deposit, the bank gives you a receipt, called a *deposit slip*.

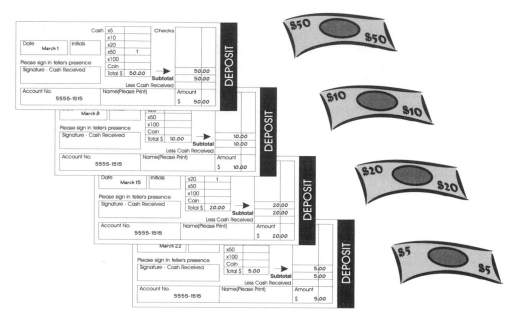

Now record these deposits in your register. We've done two of the deposits for you to show you how it's done. Notice how we used two lines for each deposit entry; this gives you room to add the deposit to the old balance in the right-hand column. For each entry, be sure you add the deposit to the old balance to get the new balance.

	PERSONAL SAVINGS ACCOUNT RECORD			
DATE	TRANSACTION	DEPOSIT (+)	WITHDRAWAL (-)	BALANCE
				0.00
3/1	Opening Deposit	50.00		50.00
				50.00 ←Add old balance
3/8	Deposit	10.00		10.00 ←to deposit
				60.00 ←to get new balance.

The last number in the right-hand column is your balance. You should have $85.00 in your account. (If you don't, check your addition.)

Step 2: Record the Interest

At the end of the month, your bank sends you a *statement*. This sheet of paper is a copy of *their* record of your account activity. It lists all deposits, withdrawals, and the interest you have earned. Compare the bank's statement with your register to be sure they have recorded all your transactions.

You need to make one more entry in your register: interest. As we showed earlier, calculating the interest on your account can get kind of complicated. The bank uses a computer to track your account activity and calculate the interest accordingly. It was the bank's computer that printed the statement.

DATE	TRANSACTION	DEPOSIT (+)	WITHDRAWAL (-)	BALANCE
3/31	Interest	0.25		0.25
				85.25

The statement shows that you've earned an incredible *25 cents* for the month! Okay, so it's not much, but it's a start. Treat the interest like a *deposit* and enter it in your register.

Now your register shows an account balance of $85.25. Pretty simple, isn't it? You'll be using this kind of account register in the next few chapters to track other accounts.

HE'S WATCHED MARY POPPINS FAR TOO MANY TIMES!

BANK

BUT I WANT TO FEED THE BIRDS!!

Bank Words

annual percentage rate:	(APR) the interest rate the bank pays over one year
balance:	the total principal and interest in your account
compound interest:	interest that's paid on the principal and any interest earned so far
interest:	fee banks pay depositors for the use of their money
principal:	any money you deposit in the account (as opposed to interest, which the bank pays into your account)
register:	paper form used to record your account activity: deposits, withdrawals, interest payments
simple interest:	interest that's paid on the principal only
statement:	computer-printed copy of bank's record on your account for one month
transaction:	any change made in your account, such as a deposit or withdrawal
yield:	the amount of interest your investment produces, figured as a percentage of the investment

Changing Your Future

Many teenagers treat their long-term savings account as a *spending* account. They store their money there for a few weeks or months, then take it out to spend it on something. This is a bad habit, and it only gets worse as they grow older.

Someday, they'll need a large chunk of money to buy a car or pay for college or start a business. But if they've been keeping a "spending account," most of their money will have been spent on shoes, CDs, clothes, video games, fast food, sports equipment, and a hundred other small and less-important things. Instead, they should keep a long-term savings account for goals like college or a car and a short-term savings account for smaller goals. Otherwise, their only choice is to *borrow* the money for what they need. Now instead of *earning* interest from the bank on all that money, they're *paying* interest to the bank! It doesn't have to happen this way.

Believe it or not, you can change the course of your future—in a big way—*right now*. You can save yourself thousands of dollars. You can make it possible to afford the big stuff you really need and spend the rest of your life being glad that you took the right steps, *if* you do what is suggested in the activity on page 25.

You don't have to put *all* your money in the long-term account! Just put *something* in the account every week—even a dollar or two, if that's all you can afford.

Just get in the consistent habit of setting aside some of your money. It may not seem like much, and you won't get rich on the interest; but, over a period of time, you'll accumulate enough money to do something significant. And the interest you save on loans in your future (loans you won't need!) *will* make you rich!

In Chapter 5, Keeping Track of All That Money, we'll show you how to budget your money so you can have spending money *and* a growing savings account. But the first step is to start saving now, even if you don't have much. And if you're already making regular deposits, good job! Chapter 8, Making Money with Money, will show you how to make the most of your investment.

Extra, Extra

If you don't already have a long-term savings account, open one this week.

Start a register of your account activity and keep it current by entering all transactions and interest payments.

Ask your bank for information on your account: the annual percentage rate, the yield, and how often they compound the interest—whether daily or monthly.

Start Banking

1. Go to your local bank and open a short-term or long-term savings account. (Ask your parents to help you find one that caters to youth bankers. Some banks have accounts with special interest rates and features for young people.)

2. To get in practice for your real account, set up a mock bank system with your parents. The goal is to see how the banking system works. Make photocopies of the check, deposit slip, withdrawal slip, and account registers in the back of this book.

    a. Ask your parents to deposit your allowance into your mock account.

    b. Write out a deposit slip for the amount you are paid.

    c. Record the amount in your account register.

    d. When you want some cash, make out a withdrawal slip for the amount you want.

    e. Record the withdrawal in your account register, entering it in the "withdrawal" column.

    f. Keep a running total or balance.

Rewind

1. Banks are in the money business: they borrow the money from depositors at lower interest and lend it to borrowers at higher interest.

2. There are two types of interest: *simple interest* and *compound interest.*

3. Simple interest is paid only on the *principal* (your investment).

4. Banks pay compound interest, which is paid on the principal *and* any interest earned so far.

5. Use an account register to keep track of all account activity: deposits, withdrawals, and interest payments.

6. Banks send monthly *statements* to show you their record of your account activity. Always compare your register with the statement to be sure everything is correct. Record your interest payment in the register—it's listed on your statement.

7. A long-term savings account is for saving, not spending. Make regular deposits and keep your money in the bank until it's time to make a major investment.

8. A short-term savings account is for goals that take a few months to save for.

9. Keep some money for fun and entertainment—your "spending" money.

notes

_____

_____

_____

_____

_____

_____

_____

_____

CHAPTER 3

The Checkbook

Chapter 3

The Checkbook

In this lesson you'll learn all about checking accounts—why they were invented, how they work, and how to make deposits. You'll even learn how to write your own checks, using the blank checks we've provided for you in this book.

Most important of all, you'll learn how to keep a running record of your checking account (so you'll always know how much money you have—or don't have). Checking accounts are easy to understand and simple to use. Let's see how.

Permission Notes for Banks

A check is really just a *permission note*: It gives your bank permission to take money from your account and give it to someone. Here's how it works.

Let's say that you're sitting around the house watching another *Gilligan's Island* rerun and wishing there was something fun to do. Just then, you spy a catalog from The Great Big Boat Company on the coffee table. As you look through the catalog, you spot the yacht of your dreams—on sale for only $1 million (and that *includes* the anchor!). You decide to buy it.

The money is no problem—you have several million dollars in your bank account. But you must figure out a way to get *one million* of those dollars safely from the bank to the boat seller.

You *could* go to your bank after school, withdraw one million dollars ($1,000,000.00), and take the money to the boat seller. But it's not smart to carry that much money around. And besides, the company is all the way across the country—and you've got school tomorrow. You *could* withdraw the cash, stick it in a box, and mail the money to the boat seller. But if the box were lost or stolen, you would be up a creek—without your boat.

Solution? Write a permission note *addressed to your bank* and send it to the boat seller (don't forget to sign it!).

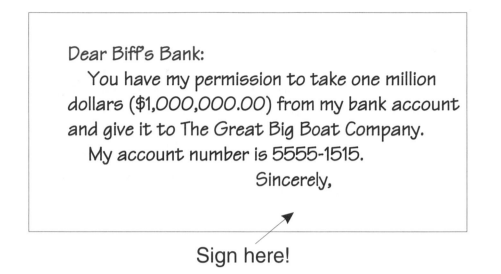

Dear Biff's Bank:
    You have my permission to take one million dollars ($1,000,000.00) from my bank account and give it to The Great Big Boat Company.
    My account number is 5555-1515.
                  Sincerely,

Sign here!

When The Great Big Boat Company gets your permission note (along with the yacht-order form), they take it to your bank. The folks at the bank withdraw $1 million from your account and give it to the boat seller (now your balance is only $5 million). Then The Great Big Boat Company sends you your new yacht.

To make things easy for everyone, banks make official permission notes, called *checks*, with most of the information already printed on the form. All you do is fill in the blanks and sign it.

The payee

142

Date _____

Pay to
the order of _____ $ [_____]

_____ Dollars

Some Bank
Someville, USA
Account #12345-6789
  I: 1232958789 I: 123958 IO2

_____

Amount (in words)   Amount (in numbers)

Sign here!

The check contains the same information as the permission note: your name and account number, the *payee* (who the bank pays the money to), the amount, the date, and your signature.

To make things even more convenient, banks have an agreement to accept each other's checks. This way, The Great Big Boat Company doesn't have to go to your bank to get the money. They just "cash" the check at *their* bank—Sid's Savings. Then Sid's Savings sends the check to Biff's Bank, who withdraws the money from your account and gives it to the other bank.

(Actually, it's more complicated than that: Both banks have an account at the Federal Reserve Bank—the bank for banks. The Federal Reserve Bank transfers the money from Biff's Bank to Sid's Savings.)

Checks can be a convenient way to pay for things. They are safer to carry than cash and safer to mail. But checks also can get you into trouble. When you write a check, you are making a promise. You are promising the *payee* (the person you're giving the check to) that you have the cash in your bank account.

If you don't, the bank will refuse to "honor" it (cash the check). This means you have "bounced" the check—instead of being converted to cash, it "bounces back" into the payee's hands unpaid. The person you owe (payee) is left with a worthless piece of paper, and you've broken your promise.

Most bounced checks are caused by people who don't keep an accurate record of their checking account. They think they have the money to cover the check, but there's not enough money in their account to honor the promise. In the next chapter you'll learn more about how to avoid bouncing a check. But first, let's practice using a checking account.

Step 1: Make a Deposit

You've just opened a checking account at Biff's Bank. Your checkbook contains checks, deposit slips, and a check register for keeping track of your transactions. You have no money in the account yet, so let's make a deposit. You've been helping some of your neighbors with some heavy-duty yard work and they've paid you with checks: one for $60 and another for $40.

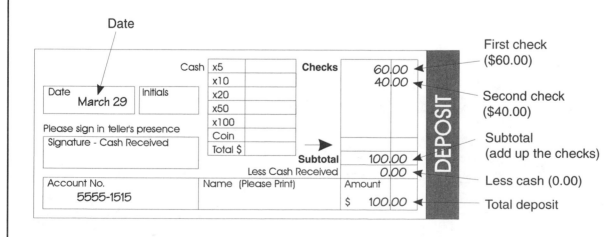

To deposit these checks into your account, fill out a deposit slip taken from the back of your checkbook.

Now turn to the *register* in the front of the checkbook and record the deposit.

			PAYMENT DEBIT (-)	FEE (IF ANY) (-)	DEPOSIT/ CREDIT (+)	BALANCE
NUMBER	DATE	DESCRIPTION OF TRANSACTION				0.00
	Mar 29	Deposit - Yard work			100.00	100.00
						100.00

Caption above table: RECORD ALL CHARGES OR CREDITS THAT AFFECT YOUR ACCOUNT

Right margin notes:
Write deposit amount here too

Add the deposit to your previous balance ($0.00) to get the new balance.

Amount of the deposit

Check no.
    Today's date
        "Deposit - Yard work"

Your check register is the most important part of your checkbook. Always write every transaction in it. Right now your register should show $100 as the last number in the right-hand column. That's your *balance*: you have $100 in your account. It's not enough to buy that yacht, but it is enough to pay for some things you need to take care of right away. Let's write some checks.

Step 2: *Write and Record Checks*

You have three checks to write for this exercise. The first check goes to the Mission Fund, as a $20 donation to a special project at your church. The second check goes to your mom, who lent you $10 last week and you want to pay her back. The third check goes to The Spiffy Sweatshirt Company for the cool sweatshirt you ordered from them for $25.

Yes, I support our student missionaries on this special project.

☐ $10.00   ☑ $20.00   ☐ $30.00

Please make checks payable to "Mission Fund"

Pay back Mom $10.00

SPIFFY SWEATSHIRT COMPANY

ITEM	SIZE	PRICE/UNIT	NO. UNITS	PRICE
Cool Sweatshirt	XL	$20.00	1	$20.00

SHIPPING & HANDLING	$5.00
TOTAL	$25.00

Please make checks payable to "Spiffy Sweatshirt Company."
(Allow 5 weeks for delivery.)

Here are three checks pulled from your checking account and your check register showing your $100 balance. We've written and recorded your first check so you can see how it's done. (But be sure to sign and date the check!) Go ahead and write the next two checks. Be sure to record the information in your register, and *subtract* the check amount from your old balance to get your new balance.

Your Name
Your Address
001
Date _____

Pay to
the order of ___Mission Fund_____ $ | 20.00 |

___Twenty_____ 00/100 Dollars

Biff's Bank
Biffville, USA
Account #55555-1515

_____(Sign Here)_____

I: 1232958789 I: 123958   102

Your Name
Your Address
002
Date _____

Pay to
the order of _____ $ | |

_____ Dollars

Biff's Bank
Biffville, USA
Account #55555-1515

_____

I: 1232958789 I: 123958   102

Your Name
Your Address
003
Date _____

Pay to
the order of _____ $ | |

_____ Dollars

Biff's Bank
Biffville, USA
Account #55555-1515

_____

I: 1232958789 I: 123958   102

activity · activity · activity · activity · activity · activity · ac

		RECORD ALL CHARGES OR CREDITS THAT AFFECT YOUR ACCOUNT				
NUMBER	DATE	DESCRIPTION OF TRANSACTION	PAYMENT DEBIT (-)	FEE (IF ANY) (-)	DEPOSIT/ CREDIT (+)	BALANCE
						0.00
		Deposit - Yard work			100.00	100.00
						100.00
001		Mission Fund	20.00			-20.00
						80.00

Are all three checks completed, dated, and signed? Are all three recorded properly in your register? Is your running balance in the right-hand column complete? Your new balance should be $45. If it's not, go back and check your subtraction.

Keeping a checking account takes some work. You've got to record every deposit and every check and keep an accurate balance in that right-hand column. It takes a few moments to do it right. But it's not nearly as much work as writing individual permission notes to your bank or going to the bank each time you need to give money to someone.

Here's the best part: If you can keep accurate records in a register, you can handle just about any "accounting" task! Later on in the book, we'll show you how to track *all* your money: how much you earn, save, give, and spend. You can do it . . . if you know how to keep a register.

Extra, Extra

Ask a parent if you can write some checks for them. Fill out the checks (but don't sign them!) and record everything in the check register.

Why People Use Checks

- safer to use than cash
- safer to mail
- more convenient than going to the bank every time you need to pay someone
- canceled checks provide a record of your spending

Open your own checking account.

Start "Checking"

Open your own checking account. If you want more practice in check writing, ask your parents if you can complete some checks for them.

1. Remember not to sign the checks; your name is not on the account so the bank would not accept it.

2. Fill in their check register with the correct amounts and who the checks were for.

3. Calculate the balance in the account. Check your math.

one...two...three...four

Why do people write out the numbers on checks ("four hundred dollars"), rather than just use the numbers ($400)? There are two reasons.

1. An unscrupulous person might be tempted to add a zero to a handwritten "$400" and cash *your* check for $4,000. That's not so easy to do when you write out the numbers: you can't make "four hundred" look like "four thousand."

2. By writing the amount twice—once in numbers and once in letters—there's less confusion about the amount. Is that a 1 or a 7? Is that a decimal point or a comma? The written amount settles any confusion.

Check Words

activity:	changes in the account balance, including deposits, withdrawals, checks cashed, service fees
bounced check:	a check the bank returns to payee unpaid because the account didn't contain enough money to cover it
NSF:	Not Sufficient Funds—the bank's polite way of saying the check bounced—not enough money in the account
payee:	the person or company you wrote the check to
register:	printed form used to record your transactions

Rewind

1. A check is a permission note: It gives your bank permission to take money from your account and give it to someone.

2. A check is a promise: You're promising the payee that you have money in your account to cover the check.

3. A "bounced" check returns to the payee unpaid because the writer of the check doesn't have enough money in the account to "honor" the check.

4. Most people who bounce checks do it because they don't keep accurate records of their account.

5. The most important part of a checkbook is the register.

6. The most important step to writing a check is recording the information in the register.

7. If you can handle a register, you can learn to track *all* your money transactions.

notes

CHAPTER 4

Reconciling Your Checking Account

Chapter 4

Reconciling Your Checking Account

When you write a check, you are making a promise. In this chapter we will show you how to keep your promise. Your bank sends you a record of your account each month. Since they're the ones holding your money, it's very important to be sure that their record matches your register. You'll learn how to reconcile these two documents to keep your account—and your reputation—healthy.

Reconcilable Differences

In the previous chapter you learned how to make a deposit, write checks, and record these transactions in your check register. There's one more critical step to managing a checking account: *reconciling*.

Reconciliation is an idea you're already familiar with. Let's say that you and a friend have a disagreement. Sooner or later (sooner is better!), you talk about it, shake hands or hug, and settle your differences. In other words, you've reconciled.

When you reconcile your *checking account*, you settle any disagreement between your checkbook register and the bank's records on your account. Like you, the bank keeps a record of all the activity in your account—deposits, withdrawals, checks cashed. And lots of times, their records add up to something different than your records. To be sure your relationship with the bank stays strong, you have to reconcile any disagreement in each other's records. Why would there be a disagreement? There are three main reasons.

1. Errors. It's pretty easy to make a math error, and maybe you subtracted wrong. Or you forgot to record a check and you think you have more money in your account than you do. Or maybe the bank made an error—they make mistakes too.

2. Charges. Your bank may charge you a fee for keeping a checking account, or they may charge you a few cents every time you write a check. And if you bounce a check, or order custom-designed checks, you'll be charged for these things too—and the money will be taken directly from your checking account. (You should record these in your register.)

3. The Float. You may have written a check and recorded it in your register, but the *payee* may not have cashed it yet, or the bank hasn't recorded the transaction yet. It's "floating" somewhere in the system. Until the check is cashed and deducted from your account, the bank's record shows you have more money in your account than what your register shows you have.

If, for any of these reasons, you *think* you have more money in your account than is actually there, you run the risk of bouncing a check. And that's not a good thing.

So how do you guarantee that your register matches the bank's record? The bank makes it pretty easy for you: Every month, they send you a *statement*. Your checking account statement is a copy of the bank's record of your transactions. By comparing the statement with your register, you can spot the differences and update your register to match. Here's how.

The Bank Makes a Statement

Let's say that last month you made that $100 deposit in your new account and wrote the three checks from the previous chapter. You wrote no other checks and made no more deposits. Here's a copy of your check register.

NUMBER	DATE	DESCRIPTION OF TRANSACTION	PAYMENT DEBIT (-)	FEE (IF ANY) (-)	DEPOSIT/ CREDIT (+)	BALANCE
		RECORD ALL CHARGES OR CREDITS THAT AFFECT YOUR ACCOUNT				0.00
		Deposit - Yard work			100.00	100.00
						100.00
001		Mission Fund	20.00			-20.00
						80.00
002		Mom	10.00			-10.00
						70.00
003		Spiffy Sweatshirt Co.	25.00			-25.00
						45.00

At the end of the month, the bank mailed you a statement. It lists the deposits, the checks cashed, and any other charges. It looks something like the following.

Checking Account Statement

Account Number: 5555-1515

CHECKS

date	check no.	amount
03/07	001	$20.00
03/10	003*	$25.00

OTHER ACTIVITY

date	transaction	amount
03/01	DEPOSIT	$100.00+
03/05	CUSTOM CHECKS	$10.00-
03/31	SERVICE CHARGES	$10.00-

BALANCES

OPENING BALANCE	$100.00
CLOSING BALANCE	$35.00

As you can see, they don't match. For one thing, the closing balance on the statement is $35, but your register shows that you should have *$45* in your account! No worries. Just reconcile your account to find out what happened.

Step 1: Add the Charges

The first thing you notice is that the bank charged you $10 for printing those fancy-looking checks you ordered when you opened your account. They also charged a $10 monthly fee for providing you with a checking account. Those charges don't appear in your check register, so go ahead and write them in now, just like you would record a check. Be sure to subtract each amount in the right-hand column to get your new balance.

But wait a minute. Now your register shows that you have $25; the bank says you have $35! Not a problem—just go to the next step.

Step 2: Go Through the Checks

Go back through your check register and put a check mark next to every check that was cashed. The statement shows that check numbers 001 and 003 were cashed. (See that asterisk [*] next to 003 in the statement? That's the bank's way of pointing out that there's a check missing.)

Now when you look at your statement, you see that check number 002 wasn't cashed yet. (That was the check you wrote to your mom. She was so excited about your paying her back, she put the check in her pocket and forgot about it!) Go ahead and write "$10.00" directly beneath the "$35.00" closing balance on the *statement*. Now subtract, and write down the new balance on the statement: $25.00.

Now the statement "agrees with" your check register: you've *reconciled* your account. You have $25 in your checking account—or you *will*, as soon as your mom finds that check and cashes it!

Of course, this exercise was pretty easy because you didn't have much activity in your account. Things get more complicated when you write lots of checks, make several deposits, and withdraw money directly from your account using an automatic teller machine (ATM). To make things easier for you, most banks print a little worksheet on the backs of their statements. You just fill in the blanks, do some adding and subtracting, and, surprise! You are reconciled!

Regardless of how much you use a checking account, reconciling it is a simple, step-by-step process. It's also a necessary process. You're about to find out why.

Beware the Bouncing Check

In the previous chapter we talked about the bounced check. If you write a check but don't have enough money in your account to cover it, the bank may give it back to the payee and say, "Sorry, it's no good." And it's "no good" for all sorts of reasons.

Let's say that you *didn't* reconcile your account. You still think you have $45 in the account, because you didn't write down those extra charges the bank made. You make another deposit and write a few more checks. Meanwhile your mom finds that $10 check and deposits it in *her* checking account. The next day the bank calls her to say that your check bounced. They won't give her the $10. What's worse, they're charging her $15 for the bad check. Now you still owe her $10 *plus* the $15 fee—and she wants you to pay in cash this time!

But wait: It gets worse. Your bank charges you $25 for writing the bad check. You don't know that, because you don't read your statements. Now there's even less money in your account, so it's likely that you're going to bounce *another* check. If the check you bounce was written to a store, they'll keep a record of your credit, and they might refuse to accept a check the next time you try to buy something there.

How NOT to Bounce a Check

Bouncing checks is expensive and damaging to your reputation. Follow these tips to help you avoid writing bad checks.

- Record every transaction in your register as soon as you make it.
- Reconcile your statements as soon as they arrive.
- If you can't get your account to balance, go to your bank and ask for help.
- Set your own "minimum balance" and don't allow yourself to let the account dip below that amount. This will give you a margin for error.

If you bounce a few checks in a row, your bank may close your account. They won't honor checks from a person who can't honor a promise. And if that's not bad enough, consider this: If the bank thinks that you're doing this on purpose—trying to pay for things with money you don't have—they can have you *arrested*! The moral of this lesson? Record every transaction in your check register, and reconcile your account as soon as you get your monthly bank statement.

Account Shopping

Banks generally charge fees for keeping a checking account. Some charge a monthly fee, others charge a few cents for every check written; some banks charge for both. Often, fees can be avoided by keeping a minimum balance—$100 or more. Before you open a checking account, shop around for the best deal.

If you write few checks a month, a per-check charge may be cheaper than keeping a minimum balance. That's because most checking accounts don't pay you interest on your money, so you may be better off keeping that extra $100 in your savings account.

Keeping Track

1. Carry a small notebook.

2. For a month, write down everything you spend, no matter how small.

3. This means everything: gum, soft drinks, snacks, bus fare, comics, arcade games, as well as larger purchases.

4. Even if you are spending "loose" change, write it down.

   You'll be amazed at how much you spend on little things or things you hardly think about or notice at the time. This exercise can help you feel in control of your money so you know exactly where it's all going, and you'll know exactly what you got for it.

Rewind

1. *Reconciling* your account means matching your check register with the bank's record.

2. Each month, the bank sends you a copy of their record, called a *statement*.

3. The first step to reconciling your account is to add their charges to your register.

4. The second step to reconciling your account is to subtract uncashed checks from the statement's closing balance.

5. To make reconciling easy, most banks print a work sheet on the back of the statements.

6. *Bouncing* a check can be expensive and also damaging to your reputation.

7. You can avoid bouncing checks by recording all transactions in the check register and reconciling the account with the monthly statement.

notes

CHAPTER
5
Keeping Track of All that Money

Chapter 5

Keeping Track of All That Money

So far you've learned how to manage a savings account and a checking account. Believe it or not, you now have all the skills you need to manage your money! We're about to take these skills and show you how to set up and maintain a budget, keep track of all your earning, saving, giving, and spending . . . and how to have fun doing it! Let's get started.

Money, Money, Everywhere

You're about to learn something that 90 percent of all adults haven't figured out: how to keep control of your money! We don't know how much money you make from a job or how much allowance you get, but we're sure that at least *some* money passes into and out of your wallet (or pocket or purse or wherever you keep it) every week. We're going to show you how to take charge of that process.

Let's say that you get about $20 each week from your allowance and an occasional job (baby sitting, yard work, whatever). Maybe you make a lot more than that in real life. Maybe you make less. It doesn't matter. We'll use $20 a week for this exercise to show you how simple it is to control your money.

It's kind of obvious, but we'll say it anyway: Your *average weekly income* is $20. You can save and give and spend as much as you want—as long as you don't exceed $20 a week.

Let's also say that you want to *tithe* money to your church, which means giving away a percentage of your income. We'll talk more about that in Chapter 7, Giving It Back. For now, let's say that you want to give 10 percent of your income to your church. That means you tithe $2 per week.

Let's make one more assumption: You want to set aside another 20 percent of your income for long-term savings. That comes to $4 per week.

Of the $20 weekly income, $2 goes to the church, $4 goes to long-term savings, and $14 is left over for everything else. You just created a budget. It's that simple. Making a budget is an important step, but it's just the first step. The *budget* is the plan; this is what you *intend* to do. You still need a system to carry out the plan. Here it is.

Weekly Budget	
Income	+ $20
Giving	- $2
Saving	- $4
	———
Spending	= $14

The Envelopes, Please

It's a simple system. First, we take three envelopes and label them: Giving, Long-Term Savings, Spending. These are the names of the three accounts in your system.

In a moment, you're going to divide your $20 among the account envelopes. But first, let's make a record of your earnings. It's nice to know how much money you make—and easy to forget if you don't write it down. So take a sheet of paper with some columns on it, title it "Earnings," and record what you've made.

Let's say that it's April 1, and you were given $10 for babysitting and $10 for allowance. We've recorded the first entry; you can enter the second one.

Earnings Record
For the Week of: April 1-7

DATE	INCOME SOURCE	AMOUNT
4/1	Babysitting for Jensons	$10.00

There's no need to add up your income on this record; you can do that later with a calculator if you need to know the totals sometime in the future. Working teenagers must file a return, but you pay tax only if you earned more than $4,000 in the year.

Now it's time to *deposit* the money into the accounts: $2 in the GIVING envelope, $4 in the LONG-TERM SAVINGS envelope, and $14 in the SPENDING envelope. As you learned earlier in the book, *every* deposit must be recorded in the account's register. Here are the registers for these accounts. We've recorded the GIVING deposit to show you how it's done. Go ahead and record the correct SAVINGS and SPENDING deposits in their respective registers.

GIVING ACCOUNT for week of : April 1 - 7

Date	Transaction	Deposit	Withdrawal	Balance
4/1	Deposit	2.00		2.00
				2.00

LONG-TERM SAVINGS ACCOUNT for week of : April 1 - 7

Date	Transaction	Deposit	Withdrawal	Balance

SPENDING ACCOUNT for week of : April 1 - 7

Date	Transaction	Deposit	Withdrawal	Balance

Now that the money is in the account envelopes, and you've recorded your deposits, it's time to take the money *out*. Let's say that on April 2, you take the money from the GIVING account envelope and drop it in the offering container at church. Now record the transaction in the GIVING register as a *withdrawal*. Your balance in that account should now be $0.

The LONG-TERM SAVINGS account is even easier. Just deposit the envelope's contents into your *real* savings account. This account register is your *actual* bank account register. It's not a withdrawal until you take the money out of your bank account. (That is something you're not going to do for a long time because you read Chapter 2 carefully!)

This leaves us with the SPENDING account. Every time you spend money, you write down what you spent as a withdrawal. There's only $14 in there, and it must last you all week, so be careful. For this example, we've gone ahead and spent some money *for* you! Here's what was spent— and for what. Go ahead and record each of these items as a withdrawal in your SPENDING account register on page 48.

4/2	fast food	$2.00
4/4	magazine (*Yachting!*)	$5.00
4/5	arcade	$3.00

If you subtracted correctly, you should have a balance of $4 in the right-hand column. What would you do with that extra cash? Leave it in the envelope! The next week's register would start with a $4 opening balance. Each week, you would "roll over" or "carry over" the balances, if any, from the previous week's registers, and start new registers.

If you would like to try this system for real, go ahead. Use your real savings account register for LONG-TERM SAVINGS, and create other accounts according to your own needs. We've printed a standard account register in the back of the book, which you can photocopy and label with your own account titles. You're on your own for the envelopes.

Go Ahead and Set Up a Budget

1. Calculate your average weekly income (or biweekly). $ _____

2. Divide it between the budget categories:

    Tithes/giving $ _____

    Long-term savings $ _____

    Short-term savings $ _____

    Spending $ _____

3. Write out this budget and get an envelope and account register for each priority on your budget list.

4. Begin putting your real money in your new budget!

    a. Deposit your long-term savings in your real account.

    b. Start a short-term savings account and deposit that money.

    c. Pay your tithe.

Budget Tricks

As you've probably guessed by now, if you want to make any large purchases, you're going to have to spend *less than* $14 each week and "roll over" the balance from week to week. Here's a simple way to do it.

Open a new account—a short-term savings account! This is for goals that will take several weeks or months to save for. For example, if you need to save $100 for your youth group's ski trip, adjust your budget accordingly and deposit money into an envelope marked SHORT-TERM SAVINGS: SKI TRIP. If you set aside $8 a week, you'll make your goal in 13 weeks. Time to get a raise!

If you're like most teenagers, your income varies from week to week. Not a problem. In the above example, your first two priorities, giving and long-term savings, are based on percentages. If you're committed to giving 10 percent, just divide *whatever* you make by 10 and that's how much you give that week. If you're committed to putting 20 percent of your income in your long-term savings account, divide your earnings by 20 and deposit that amount.

Maybe some weeks you make so little that there's hardly anything to spend. Welcome to the real world! This is where budget planning pays off. Smart money managers set aside money in a "Just in Case" account. (Get out another envelope!) When they come into a dry week (no money), they reach into this special account to make ends meet. If you can't count on a regular income, spend a bit less during the good weeks and keep it there until you need it.

NEW WEEKLY BUDGET		
Income	+	$20
Giving	-	$ 2
Savings	-	$ 4
Skiing	-	$ 8
Spending	=	$ 6

Here's another way to smooth out the bumps of a rocky income: Make longer-term budgets. Most adults get paid just once or twice a month, so they make *monthly budgets*. Many adults, such as real-estate brokers, salespeople working on commission, authors, and the self-employed, get no regular paychecks. These folks often make *annual budgets* because they know the money in their accounts must last for months. If *you only make an income every once in a while,* make a monthly budget and then divide up the account balances to tell you how much you can afford each week.

A Budget That Works

If you have any kind of income, you can make a budget that works. Here are the steps: First, write a budget that divides your income among your priorities. Second, create registers for each account (priority). Third, divide your earnings among your accounts and enter each amount as a deposit. And last, whenever you take money from an account, enter the transaction as a withdrawal from that account.

Your accounts may look different than our example. Your income is sure to be different. But the *system* is the same, regardless of your income and priorities. Try the system for a few weeks. We are confident that it will help you save and give more money than before, and it will keep your spending under control. See for yourself.

Rewind

1. A budget is your plan on how to divide your income among your priorities.

2. Each priority becomes an *account*. You divide your income among these accounts.

3. Each account has its own *account register*: record your deposits and withdrawals in the register.

4. "Carry over" any account's balance into the next week.

5. When your priorities change, open new accounts.

notes

_____

_____

_____

_____

_____

_____

_____

_____

_____

_____

_____

_____

_____

_____

_____

CHAPTER 6

Managing Bigger Budgets

Managing Bigger Budgets

We used a simple budget in that last chapter to show you how easy it is to keep track of your money. But what happens when you have a bigger income and dozens of monthly living expenses? This chapter will show you how the same budget and accounting system works for an adult—and how to customize it for you.

A Confession

In the previous chapter, we used envelopes to separate the money into different accounts. It's easier to understand budgets and accounting that way. Well, now that you know how to do all the fancy accounting, it's time to tell you the truth: Most folks don't keep their money in envelopes. (Okay, so you already knew that.) Here's how they do it.

Let's imagine that you have a checking account. When you received your $20, you deposited *all* of it into this single account and recorded the transaction in your check register, of course! Here's the cool part: All that money is *actually* in one account at the bank, but in your *budget* it's divided into different accounts.

That's because, even though you're not using separate *envelopes*, you are still using separate *account registers*. First, you write a check to yourself for $4 (and record it in your check register as a withdrawal) and deposit this check in your real Long-Term Savings account. You record the deposit in your Long-Term Savings register.

Next, you record a $2 deposit in your Giving register. Later that week, you'll write a check for your donation and record the withdrawal in your Giving register (and your check register—always).

Finally, you record a $14 deposit in your Spending register. Anytime you write a check, or take cash out of the ATM machine, you record the withdrawal in the spending register (and your check register . . . you get the point).

This seems like a lot of work: Why do it? Let's learn from the people who *don't* keep separate account registers. They put all their money in the checking account.

When they need to pay for something, they look at their check register. If there's money in it, they figure they can afford it. But they forget that they're trying to set aside money for the church, or for that ski trip, or rent, or food! When the bills come, their accounts are empty. They're stuck.

By keeping separate account registers, you know exactly how much of the money in your checking account is available for each priority in your life. When it is time to buy the things you need, the money will be there—assuming you earned it in the first place!

Right now you probably don't have a lot of expenditures, and you won't go hungry, naked, or homeless if you happen to mess up on your budget. But in a few years, your money management skills *will* keep food in the fridge, clothes on your back, and a roof over your head. *If you can manage a budget now, managing your budget in the future will be much easier.*

An Adult Budget

When you get older, you can use this same budget system. Just open new accounts as you need them: Housing, Food, Clothing, Auto, Insurance, Recreation (yes!), Taxes (sorry)—whatever you need to stay ahead of your money.

Most adults are paid once or twice a month instead of weekly, so they set up *monthly* budgets. Let's look at one adult's budget to see how it's done.

Carlos is 22, fresh out of college, and living on his own in an apartment. He works as a graphic artist for a publishing company and makes $24,000 a year. His monthly *gross* income is $2,000, but his *take-home* pay is only $1,500. Why? Because his company takes out about 25 percent of his income for taxes, Social Security, medical insurance, and other deductions. He receives two paychecks a month: $750 on the first day of the month, and another $750 on the fifteenth day of the month (for a monthly income of $1,500).

Carlos's budget reflects his priorities: He wants to buy a house someday, so he puts away 10 percent of his pay in Long-Term Savings: that's $150. He gives 10 percent of his gross income to the church (tithe): that's $200 (10 percent of $2,000); he also sponsors a needy child in Haiti for $25 a month for a total Giving of $225. Then there's his Housing (rent and utilities), Food, Auto expenses (gas, insurance, repairs), Recreation (fun stuff), Miscellaneous expenses, and Short-Term Savings.

Instead of using envelopes, Carlos deposits his paychecks in his checking account. But he keeps a separate Account Register for each of his budget categories. Let's take a closer look at some of his accounts.

CARLOS' MONTHLY BUDGET	
Take-home pay	+ $1500
Giving	- $ 225
Long-Term Savings	- $ 150
Housing	- $ 500
Food	- $ 300
Auto	- $ 150
Recreation	- $ 50
Miscellaneous	- $ 75
Short-Term Savings	- $ 50

Housing: His rent ($400) is due on the first of every month. His phone, electric, and water bills (about $100) are due in the second half of the month. So he knows that most of his first paycheck must be set aside for rent. The utilities (and his car insurance) come out of the second paycheck. During the summer months he spends less on utilities, so he rolls over the balance into the next month. During the winter his utility bill is higher, and his phone bill goes up with all the long distance calls made over the holidays. He covers the extra expenses with the money he rolled over from the summer months.

Food: A quick look at his food account tells him he can spend $10 a day on food. If he spends $8 for lunch, it leaves only $2 for the rest of the day. So he takes his lunch to work on most days and treats himself to a restaurant meal once or twice a week. (And if he splurges on a lobster dinner one night, he'll be eating rice and beans the rest of the week!)

Monthly Income & Expenses

Ask your parents to go over their monthly budget with you so you can see how an actual one works. Use the sample budget form here and ask your parents to explain why they allocate the amounts they do to each item. Fill in the form showing your parents' budget.

Annual Income _____
Monthly Income _____

LESS
1. Charitable Giving _____
2. Tax _____

NET SPENDABLE INCOME _____

3. Housing (30%) _____
    Mortgage (Rent) _____
    Insurance _____
    Taxes _____
    Electricity _____
    Gas _____
    Water _____
    Sanitation _____
    Telephone _____
    Maintenance _____
    Other _____

4. Food (17%) _____

5. Auto(s) (15%) _____
    Payments _____
    Gas & Oil _____
    Insurance _____
    License _____
    Taxes _____
    Maint/Repair/
      Replacement _____

6. Insurance (5%) _____
    Life _____
    Medical _____
    Other _____

7. Debts (5%) _____
    Credit Cards _____
    Loans & Notes _____
    Other _____

8. Enter. / Recreation (7%) _____
    Eating Out _____
    Trips _____
    Babysitters _____
    Activities _____
    Vacation _____
    Other _____

9. Clothing (5%) _____

10. Savings (5%) _____

11. Medical Expenses (5%) _____
    Doctor _____
    Dental _____
    Drugs _____
    Other _____

12. Miscellaneous (6%) _____
    Toiletry, Cosmetics _____
    Beauty, Barber _____
    Laundry, Cleaning _____
    Allowances, Lunches _____
    Subscriptions, Gifts _____
      (Incl. Christmas)
    Special Education _____
    Cash _____
    Other _____

TOTAL EXPENSES _____

Net Spendable Income _____

Difference _____

Automobile: He bought a good used car for cash a couple of years ago with the money he saved as a teenager, so he has no monthly loan payments (he must have read our Chapter 10 on loans!). But he has to pay for insurance, gas, and oil changes. Some months he spends more (like when he got a tune-up on his car before a drive to Florida); other months he spends less. He rolls over the balance in the less expensive months to cover the more expensive ones.

Miscellaneous: This is where he deducts money for things like a new lamp—and a visit to the emergency room for stitches when he got hurt. He doesn't know exactly what he's going to be needing this money for, but there's always some expense that comes along that can't be covered in the other accounts. If he didn't have this account, he'd be tempted to take the money from his *savings*. But that would mess up his priorities. The Miscellaneous account helps Carlos keep his budget and his priorities straight.

Short-Term Savings: This is where Carlos saves for items that take a few weeks or months to save for, like that microwave oven he's wanted or the vacation he is planning.

As Carlos' income grows (he's up for a raise soon) and his priorities and living expenses change, he can adjust his budget and create new accounts.

Another Confession

Now that you are almost an *expert* in accounting, we want to clear up a couple of things that can cause confusion.

Register or Ledger? Throughout the book we've referred to the piece of paper used for recording an account's activity as a *register*. That's what most people call that little record booklet in their checkbook. When they keep their records on a sheet of paper, they often call it an account *ledger* or account *sheet*. They may not even use paper at all. Popular personal accounting programs such as *Quicken™* and *Money Matters™* allow them to track all their accounts on computer. What you *call* your account records isn't important. What is important is that you *keep* accurate records of your accounts.

One Line or Two? Some people use *two* lines in their register/ledger/account sheet for each entry. That's what we've been doing in this book. This gives you room in the right-hand column to add or subtract the entry from the previous balance. Others use just *one* line for each entry, doing the math in their head or on a piece of scrap paper.

The first method gives you more room to write notes and lets you do the math as you write it. The second method uses less room and looks neater. Choose the method that works best for you. The *correct* method is the one that helps you keep accurate records.

Personal Accountant

As you can see, there's lots of flexibility in this accounting system. You can have three accounts or thirty accounts. You can store your money in a checkbook, envelopes, or a sock in the back of your drawer (we won't tell). You can call your account records *registers*, *ledgers*, or *account sheets*. You can use one- or two-line entries.

The important thing is that you create a budget, divide your money among the separate accounts, and record every deposit and withdrawal. If you can do these things, you can manage *any* amount of money: $10 (ten dollars) or $10,000,000 (ten *million* dollars).

Future Budget

After going over your parents' budget, think about what kind of income and budget you will need in order to move out either on your own or with a friend.

1. With your parents' help, do a mock budget for what you will need. Use the budget form at the back of the book.

2. Decide if you will get a place alone or have roommates.

3. How much money will it take you to live? You will need basically the same categories your parents' budget has (e.g., Tithes, Savings, Housing, Food, Auto (includes bus fare or car payments and gas).

4. What is the total of your mock monthly budget?

5. That's how much money you will need to make ends meet each month. The next question: what kind of job will pay that? It's something to think about.

Rewind

1. You don't need to keep separate account *envelopes*; you do need to keep separate account *registers*.

2. Bigger expenses must be carefully considered in your budget. You must ensure that the account has enough money in it at the right time of the month.

3. To stock up an account to cover a bigger bill (bike, motorcycle, television, VCR), deposit a larger portion of certain paychecks into the account. For example, deposit enough money from the first paycheck of the month to cover the big item. Use the second paycheck to cover other priorities.

4. A "miscellaneous" account can be used to cover unplanned and emergency expenses.

5. Some people call their account registers *ledgers* or *account sheets*.

6. Some people use two lines to enter transactions on their registers; others use one line. Use what works for you.

notes

Money Matters for Teens

CHAPTER 7

Giving It Back

Chapter 7
Giving It Back

Everything you've learned so far has shown you how to take control of your money. Now that you've worked, earned, saved, budgeted, and accounted for all that money, we're going to show you how to give it away! Giving money to God is one of the greatest gifts around. Get out your wrapping paper.

Managing Your Money

Imagine this: You've just landed the job of a lifetime. You've been appointed manager of a major account, overseeing the investment of *millions* of dollars of your boss's money. He's given you some instructions on the investments he prefers, but he's entrusted you with free reign over the actual investments. He trusts you to make the right decisions. What a job!

This is not a make believe situation. You already have this job. Your "boss," God, is the creator, ruler, and owner of all things, and He has chosen *you* to manage a portion of His wealth. Over your lifetime, you will handle millions of dollars—maybe *billions*. What you do with the money is your decision. It's a big responsibility.

Fortunately, He's given you instructions (you can find them in the Bible) for how He wants you to invest His money. God is a great boss, and His investment guidelines are designed to make your life happy and full of blessings. They may not make you rich, in the monetary sense, but they *will* make you rich in the things that count: faith, joy, friends, family, and the certainty that your life *matters*. God's instructions to you regarding His money are pretty simple. Let's take a look.

Instruction #1: Say Thanks

In the Old Testament, God told his people to *"Bring the whole tithe into the storehouse, that there may be food in my house"* (Malachi 3:10). *Tithe* is an Old English word meaning "tenth." God told them to *give back* 10 percent of their wealth (back then, that would have been livestock and crops) as a way of saying thanks for all that God had given them.

Nowadays, most people don't tithe with camels, cows, and corn. (For one thing, they don't fit in the collection basket.) But people *do* give 10 percent of their wealth to God's house (their church)—in money.

Tithing to your local church is an investment in the lives of the people in your community. The money you give pays for your ministers, the youth program, the building, missionaries, and every ministry your church provides. It really counts!

Believe it or not, some folks tithe *more* than 10 percent. They may give 20 percent, 30 percent, or more! Sound crazy? It's not, really. They figure it's God's money anyway. God takes care of all their needs with what's left.

Let's say you've got a good job and you're making $40,000 a year. You tithe 10 percent: $4,000. You work hard, do well, get some raises, and pretty soon you're making $80,000 a year. You want to thank God for the raises, so you tithe 20 percent—$16,000. You're still left with $28,000 more than you had before! (Of course, most people don't see it that way. They pour their extra money into bigger houses and faster cars. Just what they need—more carpet to vacuum and more speeding tickets to pay off.)

It works the other way too. For some people, to begin tithing an entire 10 percent is too much all at once. So they use a *graduated* tithe: They start smaller and work their way up as they're able.

If 10 percent is too big a chunk for you right now, start with 5 percent. Without a doubt, God will honor your faithfulness and make it possible for you to graduate to higher amounts in the future. Try 5 percent for two months; then graduate to 6 percent; then increase to 7 percent a couple of months later; and work your way to 10 percent. You'll be so surprised at how this works. You'll keep going! But you'll never know the thrill of saying thanks to God with a tithe unless you try. Do it this week.

Instruction #2: Help the Needy

One time Jesus was talking to some people who were pretty proud about their faithful tithing. He wasn't impressed. Instead, he let them know that while they were obeying the tithing instruction "[they were neglecting] *the more important matters of the law—justice, mercy and faithfulness*" (Matthew 23:23).

Tithing is important. But it's just a start. Taking care of people in need is high on God's priority list. The church takes care of some people's needs, but there are far more needy people than your local church can care for.

Jesus told a powerful story about helping the needy that leaves no doubt about the importance of this act of giving: "*For I was hungry and you gave me something to eat, I was thirsty and you gave me something to drink, I was a stranger and you invited me in, I needed clothes and you clothed me, I was sick and you looked after me, I was in prison and you came to visit me. I tell you the truth, whatever you did for one of the least of these brothers of mine, you did for me*" (Matthew 25:35–36,40).

If God feels the *pain* of every person in need (that's a lot of pain!), imagine the *joy* He feels when you help someone! Many teenagers give that joy to God and others every month. They may give regular gifts of money to organizations that help poor people; or they support ministries to inner-city kids; or they sponsor needy kids overseas with monthly contributions and letters back and forth.

Take a look inside your heart. See if there isn't a need tugging away, calling out for you to respond. Answer your heart! Giving to the needy is another way to show God how excited you are to be appointed a manager of His wealth.

Instruction #3: Give from Your Riches

In Luke, chapter 12, Jesus told a story about a rich farmer who was making plans to build some big barns to store all his harvest. (Back then, crops were like money, so barns were like bank vaults.) He figured that, with all that wealth stored up in his barns, he could kick back and live like the rich and famous.

But God said to him, *"You fool! This very night your life will be demanded from you. Then who will get what you have prepared for yourself?"* Jesus finished the story with this warning: *"This is how it will be with anyone who stores up things for himself but is not rich toward God"* (Luke 12:21).

When God calls somebody a fool, it's wise to sit up, pay attention, and figure out why! God had just blessed this guy with a great crop. But instead of figuring out how he could share this blessing with others, his only plan was to keep it all to himself for the rest of his life (which wasn't long!). It was like a slap in God's face.

Do a Bible Study on Tithing

1. Get a concordance and look up the following words. Write down key verses for each. Then write something the verses teach you about the terms.

Tithe

References: _____

Notes: _____

_____

_____

Giving

References: _____

Notes: _____

_____

_____

Freewill Offering

References: _____

Notes: _____

_____

_____

First Fruits

References: _____

Notes: _____

_____

_____

2. Calculate 10 percent of your weekly or monthly income. That's your tithe or 10 percent.

3. Begin to tithe it to your church. Take the money from your Tithing/Giving envelope each Sunday and put it in the offering plate.

4. Your church will give you a statement showing your total contributions once or twice a year.

When God blesses you in a big way, give in a big way! When you receive riches, give from your riches. That brings up an important question: What are *riches*? You can't put a dollar figure on it. You may make $1,200 one year and consider yourself rich. An adult making $12,000 a year has to struggle to make ends meet. And yet, some people with $12 *million* still want more.

People have *riches* when their bills are paid; they have food, clothes, and a place to live; and they still have some money left!

When you get a new job, a raise, or a big birthday check from your Aunt Edna, count your blessings. Don't do what that foolish farmer did. Say thanks to God again and give Him back a bigger share—above your tithe.

A Different Set of Rules

There are other instructions in the Bible, of course. If you read through the Gospel of Luke, you'll find dozens. All of God's money instructions are easy to follow, and every one of them will make your life better. It's sad, but you'll find few people following them.

In fact, most people live by money rules that often are the *opposite* of God's instructions. But if you look around your church, and in your community, you'll find some people who follow the Book (the Bible): They're thanking God, helping the needy, sharing their riches, and sacrificing. The result: They are rich where it counts, they're changing the lives of others, and God is rewarding their faithfulness. As money managers, they are doing a *good* job.

Making a Commitment

The first step to giving is to work on your tithe. Figure out how much money you make per month, on average. (If you're working from a weekly budget, base it on your weekly average.) Now you must decide what *percentage* of your income you would like to give back to God.

Next, multiply your average income by that percentage: The result is your tithe amount. That's the amount of money you commit to give each month.

Before you make the tithe promise, talk to God! Ask Him to help you decide on the amount you should give and ask Him to help you to follow through on it. If you are ready, you can fill in and sign the following pledge (promise) card.

EXAMPLE:

TITHING 10 percent on $80 average monthly income

Average monthly income:	$80
Tithe 10 percent:	X .10
Monthly tithe promise:	$ 8

Dear Lord,

    Thank you for caring for me in big and small ways. Thank you for providing me with food, clothes, and a place to live.

    Thank you for providing me with an average income of $____ per _____. By signing this note, I'm acknowledging that I'm not the owner of this money: You are. You've appointed me manager of this money and all other things you have given to me.

    I'm grateful to you for my position. To acknowledge that it's your money, and to thank you for the opportunity to manage it, I'm committed to return _____ percent to you on a regular basis. I'm making this commitment for _____ months.

    This amounts to $_____ per _____.

               Your servant, _____

               Date:_____

Look Into It

Do some "giving" research into some of the needs you've heard about. You could start by writing letters to the organization listed in this chapter, visiting local ones, or talking to people who have had some experience with them. Try to discover the following.

1. Their mission statement. Each organizations should have a declaration of its goals now and for the future—why it is doing what it is doing.

2. Some statistics on how many people the organization helps per week, month, or year.

3. What percentage of each dollar donated to the organization goes to overhead expenses or administration.

After you have done your research, talk over your findings with your parents. Pray about the needs and choose one organization to help.

What Happens When You Give

- You say, "Thanks, God!"
- You help people who really need it.
- Your gift could help someone meet Jesus.
- You get to work for the God of the universe.
- You can be satisfied in knowing that you're doing what God says.
- You get to change the world.
- The church has been succeeding for 2,000 years. You are helping it to continue for another year.
- You're being a good steward of what God has given you.
- You're acting on your confidence that God will care for your needs because He loves you.
- You're treating others generously—like God treats you.

Helping People in Need

AIDS hospices
Bible distribution programs
Bible translation ministries
Camping ministries
Child sponsorship
Day care programs
Drug and alcohol treatment programs
Evangelism ministries
Homeless ministries
Homes for abused children
Homes for battered women
Homes for unwed mothers
Hospitals
Hunger relief organizations
Inner-city ministries
Mission organizations
Pregnancy counseling centers
Prison ministries
Rehabilitation ministries
Shut-in ministries
Soup kitchens

Rewind

1. God is the owner of all things. He's appointed us to manage some of them.

2. The Bible contains God's instructions regarding His money.

3. God wants us to give back a portion of what He's given us, as a way of saying thanks. This form of giving to the church is called a *tithe*.

4. God wants us to give to the needy. Their pain is His pain, and their joy is His joy.

5. God wants us to give even more from our riches, to thank Him richly when He blesses us richly.

6. God wants us to give sacrificially as our faith increases.

How To Make Money with Money

Chapter 8

How To Make Money with Money

One of the best reasons for setting aside money for savings is that you can use that money to make more money. It's time to tell your money to "Go to work!" so that you will always have what you need, won't have to borrow, and can be generous. This chapter shows you how.

Make the Most of Your Savings

If you keep a good budget, you've got an account called Long-Term Savings. Each week or month you deposit a portion of your earnings into a savings account. Here are some tips that will help you to make the most of these savings and make money with your money. Always keep in mind the reasons for making more money:

1. It's good stewardship.

2. You will be able to use that money to meet future needs, including having money to get you ready for what God has planned for your life. For example, you will have money to go to college or trade school or start your own business when the time comes.

3. You'll have more money available to meet the needs you see in the world around you.

Tip #1: Don't Invest in Things That Go Down in Value

The money in your savings account is an *appreciating* investment. Its value is going up because you're earning interest. You are making money. If you withdraw some of that money to buy a pair of shoes, a CD, roller blades, or sunglasses, you've now made a *depreciating* investment. Its value goes down the moment you walk out of the store. You're losing money.

Where Has It Gone?

1. Take a look at where your money has been going. Make two lists:

    (a) Things you would really like to buy if you saved for it.

      1. _____
      2. _____
      3. _____
      4. _____
      5. _____

    (b) Things you've bought in the past on the spur of the moment.

      1. _____
      2. _____
      3. _____
      4. _____
      5. _____

2. Compare your lists. Which things would you rather have? Put your first list in order of priority and set some savings goals. When you have goals it's easier to say "no" to impulse buying. Remember, if you find something you really like it can be added to your list in the right spot.

3. Now choose a short-term savings goal, something that you really want, and begin saving toward it. It could be a special trip or an item.

    a. You'll need to do research to find the best price so that you'll know how much money you must save for your item.

    b. Don't forget to include all the costs. For example, if you want to buy a pet, you need to save for the expected veterinarian costs (like vaccinations), a leash, food dish, and so on. If it's a skateboard, you'll need a helmet and pads.

    c. Take all your costs into account, including ongoing ones such as pet food and treats. Don't forget to include taxes!

      (1) Item cost _____
      (2) Extra items needed _____
      (3) Safety items needed _____
      (4) Ongoing maintenance costs _____
      (5) Taxes _____

<table>
<tr><td colspan="2">Personal Stereo</td></tr>
<tr><td>new price:</td><td>$100</td></tr>
<tr><td>used price:</td><td>- 25</td></tr>
<tr><td></td><td>_____</td></tr>
<tr><td>depreciation:</td><td>= $75</td></tr>
<tr><td>opportunity cost:</td><td>+ $ 5</td></tr>
<tr><td></td><td>_____</td></tr>
<tr><td>Total Cost (1 year):</td><td>= $80</td></tr>
</table>

Let's say you buy a new personal stereo for $100. A year later, the stereo is worth about $25 when you sell it to your little brother. You get a year's worth of music out of it. (Actually, you only used it ten times because you couldn't afford to keep replacing the batteries; but let's not quibble.)

Let's count the cost.

A year's worth of use cost you $75. The difference between what you paid for it and what you sold it for is called *depreciation*. It's a polite way of saying you lost money.

But wait! There's another loss. You *could* have put the $100 in a long-term savings account instead. If you had done that, you might have earned about $5 in interest. You missed out on that opportunity because you invested in the stereo. This $5 is called *opportunity cost*.

Let's add it up: $75 in depreciation plus $5 in opportunity cost equals $80. Your year of stereo use cost $80 from savings.

Now $80 may not seem like a big deal. But in a few years, that $80 would have earned even more interest, and the loss would be about $100. Also, if you get in the habit of using your long-term savings account for depreciating investments, there won't be enough money in there when it's time to buy a car or pay for college. (Instead, have a short-term savings account for things like stereos and skateboards.)

Spending your long-term savings on depreciating items is like trying to walk up the *down* escalator. You work twice as hard to get to the top. Keeping your money in the savings account is like standing on the *up* escalator. You get to the top faster, with less effort.

The simple point is this: Use the money in your long-term savings account for *appreciating* investments. Use the money in your spending or short-term savings account to buy things that *depreciate* (go down) in value.

Tip #2: Never Borrow Money to Pay for Things That Go Down in Value

The fastest way to lose money is to buy a depreciating item with *borrowed* money. Let's buy that personal stereo again. But this time, pay for it with a credit card. You lose $75 in depreciation. There's still an opportunity cost because your monthly payment ate up the money you usually set aside for savings. Those

<table>
<tr><td colspan="2">Personal Stereo</td></tr>
<tr><td>new price:</td><td>$100</td></tr>
<tr><td>used price:</td><td>-$25</td></tr>
<tr><td></td><td>_____</td></tr>
<tr><td>depreciation:</td><td>= $75</td></tr>
<tr><td>opportunity cost:</td><td>+ 3</td></tr>
<tr><td>interest:</td><td>+ 10</td></tr>
<tr><td></td><td>_____</td></tr>
<tr><td>Total Cost (1 year):</td><td>= $88</td></tr>
</table>

small, monthly deposits *would have* earned you about $3 in interest. Borrowing money still attacks your long-term savings.

Then there's a *finance charge*. By the time you paid off the credit card balance (you took all year), you paid about $10 in interest. Your stereo use cost $88. Now that may not seem like a lot, but most people don't buy just personal stereos with borrowed money.

They buy all sorts of depreciating items: cars, furniture, boats, TVs, vacations, *big* stereo systems—anything that can be charged on plastic or financed with a loan. They end up paying *thousands* of extra dollars in finance charges (interest). In some cases, they're still paying for a thing long after the thing is worthless!

When you buy a depreciating item with borrowed money, you are standing on the *down* escalator. You *never* get to the top.

What's the solution? If you must buy a depreciating item, *don't* borrow the money. Instead, set aside a portion each month from spending for this short-term savings goal and buy it when you have enough to *pay cash*.

Check Out Some Savings Account Information

1. If you save $50 a month (or $600 a year) with simple interest at 10 percent per year, how much will you have at the end of 10 years?

   Use the formula: (amount of deposit + deposit x interest rate) x number of years = balance.

   NOTE: Use the decimal interest rate: 10 percent is 0.10 and 15 percent is 0.15. ($600/year + previous year's balance = new balance + $60 [which is the interest] = new year's balance)

   Year 1: ($600 + [600 x 0.1]) x 1 year = (600 + 60) x 1 = $660
   Year 2: ($600 + 60) x 2 years = $1,320
   Year 3: $660 x 3 =_____
   Year 10: _____

   If you had made your deposits and earned no interest, you would have $6,000 in the bank. But the interest on your account means you have made an extra $600!

2. If your deposits were made into a compound interest account at 10 percent for 10 years, what would it work out to?

   (Use the formula: balance + new deposit [$600] = new balance + [new balance x interest rate] = total balance.)

   Year   1: $600 + (600 x 0.1) = $660
   Year   2: $660 + 600 = 1,260 + (1,260 x 0.1) = 1,260 + 126 = $1,386
   Year   3: $1,386 + 600 = 1,986 + 198.6 = $2,084.60
   Year   4: $2,084.60 + 600 = 2,684.60 + 268.46 = $2,953.06
   Year   5: $2,953.06 + _____
   Year   6: _____
   Year   7: _____
   Year   8: _____
   Year   9: _____
   Year 10: _____

   With a compound interest account, instead of $600 you now have earned even more interest!

   Which account is the better way to go?

Tip #3: Save Every Month

Some people wait until they start to make lots of money before putting money into a savings account. But when that time comes, they have no savings habits. They continue to do what they've *always* done: Spend all of their paycheck and have nothing left.

Now is the time to start saving a percentage of every dollar you earn. Those regular weekly or monthly deposits do two things: First, they teach you a habit you'll be thankful for—for the rest of your life! Second, they *add up*! Those small monthly deposits will grow as your income grows. In a few years, those deposits, plus the interest, will buy you a clean used car, help you through college, or get you started in your own business.

Let's go back to the escalators. Every time you make a savings deposit, you're taking a step up the *up* escalator. With this little extra effort, you get to the top quicker. Start taking those regular steps *now*. Whatever your income, you can afford to put a portion of it into long- and short-term savings.

Rewind

1. Make money so you won't need to borrow and to meet your needs and the needs of others.

2. Avoid spending money on things that go down in value.

3. Don't borrow money to pay for things that go down in value.

4. Make regular deposits to your savings.

notes

_____

_____

_____

_____

_____

_____

notes

_____

_____

_____

_____

_____

_____

_____

_____

_____

_____

_____

_____

_____

_____

_____

_____

_____

_____

_____

_____

_____

_____

_____

CHAPTER 9

How To Spend Money Wisely

Chapter 9

How To Spend Money Wisely

You now have a carefully crafted budget and an account system to maintain your budget. In this chapter you'll learn some tricks and tips that will help you get the most out of every dollar in your SPENDING account. Let's go shopping!

The Selling Game

Imagine a board game called *Consumer Madness*. Players in the game are divided into two groups. Those in the first group are called *sellers*; those in the second group are called *consumers* (buyers). The sellers compete with each other to get all the consumers' money by selling them stuff. The buyers compete with each other to spend the least amount of money on the stuff they buy.

The game gets pretty wild: The sellers are shouting, "Buy *my* stuff! You need it! You've gotta have it! It'll make you cool! It's on sale! Big discounts! Low prices!"

Meanwhile, the consumers are shopping around, deciding what they want, and spending all their money before the end of the game. Then they borrow more money and spend that too.

In this game, the consumers usually lose.

You guessed it: *Consumer Madness* isn't a board game. It's a *real* game, played every day in America with real money. The sellers are the tens of thousands of companies that market stuff to teenagers. They sell shoes, clothes, CDs, movies, food, candy, drinks, deodorant, makeup, magazines, sports equipment, stereos, and video and computer games.

These marketers (sellers) spend *billions* of dollars in advertising. They sponsor TV shows, buy ad space in magazines, conduct giant marketing surveys, and employ hundreds of people to figure out how to get *you* to buy their stuff. It's no wonder that they're winning!

Most teenagers (and adults, for that matter) don't have nearly as much skill at *buying* as the marketers have at *selling*. It's a lopsided game. However, you can make the game more fair. By learning how the marketers play *their* side of the game, you can improve your performance on *your* side of the game. The result? You aren't tricked into buying things, you'll have more money to do the things you want to do, and you'll *take control* of your finances, buying decisions, and values.

Marketing people use tricks to get you to buy something. We'll look at those and also at what you can do to be sure you're getting what you want at the best price.

Trick #1: Big Discount!

The most common selling lure is to play tricks with prices. To understand price tricks, first you need to understand what "price" means. In many countries, the government and big businesses regulate (or set) prices for things.

Regulated prices mean, for example, that a loaf of bread costs the same no matter where you shop. If they set prices on milk, a gallon is the same price at every store. And if they fix the price on cassettes and CDs (compact discs) at the music stores, shopping around for the best price is a waste of time—it's the same in all the stores. The United States is not like that.

With very few exceptions, regulating or "fixing" prices is illegal in America. We have what economists call a "free-market economy." It's a fancy way of saying that people are allowed to sell things at whatever price they want. That means that a company that makes CD players can offer their merchandise to retail stores at whatever price they choose. Likewise, a store can offer to sell CD players to consumers at whatever price it chooses.

In either case, if the price is too high, people won't buy their CD players. So they try to come up with a price that is low enough for people to buy and high enough to cover their costs and allow them to make a profit.

When an electronics store advertises CD players at a "25 percent discount," your first question should be, "What price are they discounting?" Typically, they're saying that their price is 25 percent less than the *manufacturer's suggested retail price*. What's *that*? The suggested retail price (MSRP) is a price the manufacturer comes up with. It's *suggested* because it's illegal for the manufacturer to *demand* retailers to sell things at a certain price. (A free market means they're free to set their own prices.)

The suggested retail price isn't a very official number. Almost no store sells a popular item at that price: They just use that price so they can claim that their real price is so much lower!

It gets even sneakier. The "25 percent discount" doesn't *have* to be based on the suggested retail price. Let's say that the MSRP for this particular CD player is $100. If it wants to, the store can offer the CD player for $150! They'll sell a few of them at that price to people who don't know enough to shop around. The next week, the store can mark down the price a whopping 25 percent—and sell them for $112.50.

Meanwhile, a store down the street is offering the same CD player "on sale" for the same 25 percent discount—but their discount is based on the $100 SRP. Their price: $75!

Sound deceiving? It is. Here's how to cut through the confusion: Ignore "Suggested Retail Price." Ignore "On Sale!" and "Marked Down!" and "Discount!" Just compare the real, walk-out-the-door prices. The rest is just marketing hype, designed to fool you.

Shop Around

1. Choose something to research and buy (perhaps your short-term savings goal).

2. Shop around to get the best price.

3. Find someone who owns the thing you are saving for and ask for his or her advice.

You'll have lots of time to do this while you're saving toward your goal. By the time you have saved your money you will know exactly what to buy, where you can get it, and how much to spend. Follow the "wise buying" tips, and when you're sure you have the best price buy it and enjoy it!

Trick #2: Buy Now!

The quickest way to get you to buy something is to keep you from thinking about it first. The supermarket checkout stand is a great example. You know you shouldn't buy that candy bar; you're there to buy groceries. But it's practically *jumping* off the shelf. If you had time to think about it, you'd say, "No, I don't need it." But the checker is just about to total your purchases, so you throw it on the checkout counter and pay for it without thinking. (And if you're *really* impulsive, you also bought that tabloid with the headline, "ROCK STAR ADOPTS BABY FROM MARS.")

Sellers do all sorts of things to get you to buy before you've had a chance to think about it. They crowd their checkout stands with junk food and trinkets. They display candy and toys on low shelves so impulsive "cart jockeys" (little kids in shopping carts) will see and grab. They tell you there's a "limited quantity" so you'll buy it immediately, without considering the cost. (Except for God's love, there's a limited quantity to *everything*!)

For the same reason, sellers offer one-day and weekend sales, or they tell you they'll give you a "special deal"—if you buy today. They know that if you walk out of the store, you may decide you don't need it after all.

There's nothing wrong with these tactics—if you owned a store you'd want to increase your sales too. But right now you're a consumer, not a seller, so it's smart to know how to resist impulse buys. Try the following tips.

- Keep your hands in your pockets in the checkout line. It works!

- Take only enough money with you each day to cover your *needs*. You can't buy what you can't pay for.

- Set a "7 over 7" rule: Before buying anything that costs over $7, you must wait seven days. If you still want it a week later, you can buy it.

- When a salesperson pressures you with the fact that there are "only a few left," say that you'll leave the item so that someone who needs it more than you do can buy it.

Trick #3: Save!

Sellers know that many people feel a little guilty when they spend money. And just about everyone feels good when they get a good deal. So they distract you from how much you're *spending* and congratulate you on how much you're *saving*. This is where the "discount price" really comes in handy—the old price was $100, the new price is $75: "Save $25!"

Let's set things straight. You're not *saving* anything. You're *spending*. You may be spending *less*, but you're still spending. The only time you're saving is when your money is in your Savings account.

When you see those red tags shouting out the amount of money you're saving, ignore them. Look at the price. That's what you're going to *spend*, and that's what counts in your budget.

Flexible Price Tags

PRICE	WHAT IT MEANS
wholesale price (cost):	what the manufacturer charges the retailer—it varies with supply and demand and quantity ordered
manufacturer's suggested retail price (MSRP):	what the manufacture claims the product is worth—typically used by retailer as a base for discounts
sale price, discount price:	marketing hook used by retailers to encourage sales—may be a low price, or simply a discount from an inflated price
real price:	what it actually costs you to buy the product

Learn How Marketers Play Their Side of the Game

1. Ask adults, especially parents who do a lot of shopping, about the traps and gimmicks.

2. You could check out some books or magazines from the library that expose fraud and marketing scams.

3. Compare marketing campaigns. Watch commercials and notice advertizing posters. Which do you think use good marketing practices and which use gimmicks and hype?

Remember that good marketing will make you aware of the quality and usefulness of products without deception or high pressure sales tactics. A good sales campaign gives you the information—not the hype.

Rewind

1. Sellers are very serious in their efforts to get you to part with your money. Good money management can help you hold onto more of your money and get better deals on what you spend.

2. Sellers may set a higher price, then use it to claim that the *real* price is a discount. Ignore the percentages and compare real prices.

3. Sellers often arrange merchandise and make limited-time and limited-quantity offers to encourage impulse buying. Control your impulsive nature by putting off buying decisions until you've had time to think about them.

4. Sellers can distract you from how much you're spending by focusing on how much you're "saving." Ignore what you might be saving. *Think about how much you are spending.*

notes

notes

How Loans Work

Chapter 10

How Loans Work

Loans are tricky things. Lenders use their own vocabulary and some pretty tricky math. In this chapter we'll teach you some words, show you the lenders' arithmetic, and help you understand the wild world of borrowing.

Money for Rent

Let's say that some friends invite you to go skiing for the weekend. Problem: You have no skis or boots—and buying new gear will cost you $500. Do you say no and stay at home that weekend? Probably not. That's because you found a store that will *rent* you the skis and boots for just $30.

When you rent the skis, you don't own them. What you're "buying" is the *right to use* the thing for a limited time—the weekend. The owner of that equipment (the ski shop) sells you that right by charging you a rental fee. Nowadays you can rent just about anything: movies, mansions, moving vans, Mazda Miatas. You can even rent *money*.

Money rental works a lot like other rentals, just with different words. The owner of the money (the *lender* or *creditor*) sells you (the *borrower*) the right to use its money for a limited time (the *term*). The rental fee is called *interest*.

Lenders are in the money-rental business.

People in the money-rental business calculate their fee on a percentage of the *principal*—the amount of money you rent. Let's say you borrow $100 for one year at 12 percent interest. At the end of the year, you return the $100, plus $12 in interest. Easy, right?

Not exactly. This is where there's a big difference between renting money and renting anything else.

When you rented the skiing equipment, you got to use all the gear for the entire term—the weekend. You didn't have to give back the boots on Saturday and the skis on Sunday. But money lenders generally expect you to give back a portion of the loan each month. These monthly payments are called *installments* and this type of loan is called an *installment loan.*

Installment loans are easier for most people to handle. Rather than get stuck with one giant payment at the end of the loan, you can pay it back a chunk at a time. An installment loan is also cheaper because you pay interest only on what you still owe—not on the full amount.

You may recall that your bank divides your savings account's annual interest by 12 and pays you *monthly* interest on the balance that month. The lender of an installment loan does the same thing—in reverse.

The $100 loan at 12 percent is paid off in 12 chunks—12 monthly installments. The monthly interest for the first month is easy to figure: one percent of $100 is $1. You send the lender $1, plus a small chunk of the balance.

The next month you pay 1 percent interest on your balance, which is now less than $100 because you already paid some of it back. Each month you pay back a chunk of the principal and pay 1 percent interest on your balance. At the end of the year, you have paid back the $100 plus $6.63 in interest.

month	balance x	rate =	interest +	principal =	payment
1	$100.00	1 percent	$1.00	$7.88	$8.88
2	92.12	1 percent	.92	7.96	8.88
3	84.16	1 percent	.84	8.04	8.88
4	76.12	1 percent	.76	8.12	8.88
5	68.00	1 percent	.68	8.20	8.88
6	59.80	1 percent	.60	8.28	8.88
7	51.52	1 percent	.52	8.36	8.88
8	43.16	1 percent	.43	8.45	8.88
9	34.71	1 percent	.35	8.53	8.88
10	26.18	1 percent	.26	8.62	8.88
11	17.56	1 percent	.18	8.70	8.95
12	8.86	1 percent	.09	8.86	———
Totals			$6.63	$100.00	$106.63*

If this all looks a little confusing, that's because it is. Lenders use computers to calculate the interest and principal payments. The result is that you pay back the loan in a succession of *equal* payments. This is called an *amortized loan*. Amortized loans are repaid, or "put to death," in equal payments. (*Mortis* means death in Latin—as in *mortuary* and rigor *mortis*.)

Putting a loan "to death" sounds pretty painful. It is! Instead of *earning* interest, you're *paying* interest.

Compound Interest Loans

The above installment loan was a *simple interest* loan. You paid interest only on the principal—what you borrowed. There's another kind of loan available, but it's more complicated.

In Chapter 2, How Banks Work, we described compound interest. Your bank pays you compound interest on your savings account. Each month you earn interest

on the total balance: what you put in, plus all the interest you've earned so far. You earn interest on interest. Compound interest is a good thing when you're on the *receiving* end. It's no fun at all when you're *paying* it.

Most credit card accounts are compound interest loans in disguise. You won't have one for a while, but there are some things you should know. When you buy something with your credit card and don't pay the bill in full when it arrives, the issuer (lender) treats it as a loan (often at very high interest) and lets you pay it off monthly. If you do this a lot, you end up with a balance that can reach thousands of dollars.

Instead of making you pay off this loan in a certain amount of time (like an installment loan), the lender lets you make *minimum payments* each month. The amount of this small payment is printed on your bill, so it's pretty tempting to pay this little amount instead of paying off the whole thing. Here's the tricky part.

The interest you owe for that month may be *more* than the minimum payment. What does the lender do with the unpaid interest? They add it to your balance! The next month, you're not only paying interest on what you borrowed, you're paying interest on the interest.

What's more, you haven't even paid off a chunk of the principal. So you still owe all of it. You are making payments on your credit card balance, yet the balance is going *up*! Believe it or not, it gets even worse.

If you're late with your payment, or go over your credit limit, you're charged a fee. You guessed it—they add that to the balance too. Now you're paying interest on *everything*.

Remember the escalator illustration we used a few chapters ago? Well, now you're running up a *down* escalator—there's no way to get to the top. By the time you pay off your outrageous balance (if you ever do), you will have paid enough interest to buy *two or more* of whatever you bought in the first place. But it doesn't have to be this way. In the next chapter we'll show you how to keep a credit card under control.

Mortgage Forms

Go to your bank and ask to see a mortgage form. Read it carefully. Anything you can't understand, circle.

1. Look up unfamiliar banking terms in a dictionary.

2. Ask an adult to explain banking terms.

3. If your bank has a youth financial advisor, ask to make an appointment. Make a list of questions before you go. Ask for youth targeted banking information booklets (most banks have them).

Loan Words

amortized loan:	an installment loan that's paid off in multiple equal payments
APR:	annual percentage rate
balance:	in a credit card account, the total of all unpaid principal and interest
compound interest:	interest charged on principal and interest
finance charge:	the fees lenders charge for the use of their money, including interest, application fees, etc.
installment loan:	a loan that's paid back in several payments, or installments, rather than all at once
interest:	the fee lenders charge for the use of their money—also called finance charge
minimum payment:	the least amount of money the creditor expects you to pay; generally, enough to cover the interest, with not much left over to pay down the principal
period:	the fraction of a term used for computing interest and payments—generally one month
principal:	the amount of money you owe
revolving credit:	an open-ended loan arrangement, such as a credit card, that allows you to borrow and repay money gradually, rather than all at once.
term:	the length of a loan

Finding What's Fair

Lenders are in the business of renting money. And like any business, they do what they can to attract customers. Borrowing is enticing because it allows you to buy stuff you can't otherwise afford. Lenders capitalize on this lure by emphasizing the "low monthly payments," and they draw your attention away from all the extra money you're going to be paying in interest.

So how can you measure the true cost of a loan? Several years ago the U.S. Congress passed a law to help you. The Truth in Lending Act requires lenders to state the terms of their loans in a standard format—kind of like the nutritional information required on food labels. There are some key terms to look for.

APR: The Annual Percentage Rate tells you the rate the lender uses to figure the interest. They divide the APR by 12 to get your monthly balance.

Other Charges: These are fees and penalties you may have to pay for such things as annual fees, late payments, bounced checks, and early repayment of the loan. These things add up, so take note and be careful.

Total of Payments: This is the most important number on the loan. When the loan is done and paid for, this is the amount you will have paid. This is a sobering figure when you compare it to the *cash price*. The difference between the two is the price you pay for using someone else's money.

Amazing Loans

1. To get the idea of what it costs to borrow money, try this exercise. Let's pretend you have just borrowed $100,000 for a house at 7 percent interest. We have given you what your monthly payments would be if the loan was amortized over 30, 20, 15, and 10 years. Calculate how much that mortgage will cost you by the time you have paid it all off.

   Use the formula: monthly payment multiplied by number of payments = total amount paid minus principal (amount borrowed) = cost of the mortgage. We've calculated the 10 year cost for you. You calculate the others.

   If this $100,000 mortgage is amortized over:

	10 yrs at 7%	15 yrs at 7%	20 yrs at 7%	30 yrs at 7%
Monthly payments	$1,161.08	$898.82	$775.30	$665.30
Amount paid at end of period	$139,329.60	_____	_____	_____
Cost of borrowing	$ 39,329.60	_____	_____	_____

   10 years: $1,161.08 x 120 payments   = $139,329.60 - 100,000
                                                          = $39,329.60

   15 years: _____

   20 years: _____

   30 years: _____

2. Now think about these rates. The monthly payments are not that different between 10- and 20-year loans, but take a look at the difference in the amounts you end up paying! You pay a bit more each month and save a great deal of money!

   Which type of loan is the most cost effective?

Rewind

1. Lenders are in the money-rental business.

2. The "rental fee" is called interest. How they figure the interest makes a big difference in how much you pay.

3. An installment loan uses simple interest. You pay interest only on the portion of the principal you haven't paid back yet.

4. An amortized loan is an installment loan that's paid off in equal monthly payments.

5. A compound interest loan charges interest on principal and any unpaid interest.

6. Most credit card accounts become compound interest loans if you don't pay your bill in full.

notes

CHAPTER
11

How To
Borrow Money

Chapter 11

How To Borrow Money

Borrowing money has become a national pastime. Many Americans are in debt, and they spend much of their income trying to get out. This chapter will show you how to avoid loans you don't need and how to get a fair loan for things that matter.

The Road to Debt

Most Americans live on borrowed money. They rent other people's money to buy houses, cars, stereos, furniture, clothes, boats, vacations—anything they can buy with a credit card or bank loan. Our government and many businesses operate the same way.

But before you follow this well-traveled road into debt, you need to know what borrowing can do to your finances, relationships, and future. Here are three traps that ensnare borrowers.

Borrowing Is Expensive

As we showed you earlier, whenever you borrow money to buy something that goes down in value, you lose money. That's because you're paying interest *and* missing out on the opportunity to *earn* interest by putting those payments in your savings account instead. Meanwhile the thing you bought is going down in value (depreciating).

It's actually possible to make payments on something that's *worthless*: If you borrow money to pay for a cheap stereo or old car, you may end up making monthly payments on it even after it's in the junk heap.

With very few exceptions (we'll talk about those in a bit), you're better off saving your money for something until you can pay cash.

Borrowing Is Addictive

When you borrow money, you're really borrowing from your future. Here's why. Let's say you want to buy a new bike. That takes money. Most of us "buy" money with our time: We give our employers our time and they give us cash for it. If you had bought enough money with your time in the past, you could pay cash for that bike today.

But you didn't buy enough cash with your time, or maybe you just spent too much of that cash on shoes, CDs, and cheeseburgers. Either way, you can't "Quantum Leap" back into the past to buy more money with your time. Those hours are gone.

There's only one place you can still turn your time into cash: the future. Those hours are unspent.

If you want to ride that new bike today, you're going to have to borrow money from paychecks *you haven't earned yet.* So you borrow a few hundred dollars from your folks and promise to pay them back with money you'll earn by selling time baby–sitting or doing yard work or whatever. You've just sold off some of your future. If this is confusing, just wait. It's about to get depressing.

Flash forward a couple of years. Now you are working those hours that you sold two years ago so you could ride around on a new bike. Well, that new bike is now kind of trashed. It needs new tires, a chain, and a tune-up. But you can't afford these things because the money you earn is going straight to your parents to pay off the loan.

So where do you go to find the money to fix your bike? You guessed it: your future again. You borrow more money.

Most people live like this year after year. They spend *today* paying off the past, then mortgage the *future* to pay for the things they want today. Don't get hooked into this addiction. With very few exceptions, if you can't afford to pay cash, you can't afford to buy it.

---

*Make today pay its own way. Then save a little extra
to buy some freedom in your future.*

Borrowing Is Destructive

If you get a loan and fail to repay it according to the terms of the agreement, the lender will pursue you until you repay the money. You'll be bombarded with phone calls and letters. This is not the kind of popularity you had hoped for. The lender probably will also report your delinquency to credit reporting agencies, so getting another loan (or an apartment or a job) may become nearly impossible.

The lender can also sue you in court to force you to repay the loan. The judge can make you sell something you own to repay the debt, and he or she can *garnishee* your wages, which means your employer must deduct money from your paycheck before you get it. This judgment also will show up on your credit record. You get the picture? Failing to repay a loan is disastrous to your credit and to your freedom.

But wait—it gets worse. Even if you manage to make all your payments and avoid the wrath of the creditor, a burden of debt can mess up your family, friendships, marriage, job, education, and personal life. Every dollar of debt is a commitment to a job. As your debt increases, so must your paycheck. That usually means more hours away from other priorities.

Some of these priorities will begin to suffer: your grades drop, your relationships are strained, your spiritual life goes dry. It's no coincidence that those with the biggest debts also have trouble in their homes: Money problems place high on the list of reasons why couples divorce, so it is important to establish good habits now.

Credit Record

It's a good idea to gain some experience making regular payments and to begin developing a credit record (a history of paying what you owe). This will help you later when you have regular bills to pay or want to take out a loan for a house. Ask your parents to give you a loan to purchase something you want.

1. Have them write an agreement showing how much interest you will pay, what your weekly or monthly payments will be, and what penalties there will be if you miss payments.

    Agreement between _____ and _____

    Amount borrowed: _____

    Interest rate: _____

    Monthly/weekly payments: _____

    Penalties for missed payments: _____

    Signed _____

    Date _____

2. When you've repaid the loan in full, have your parents write a "credit history" letter stating your accomplishment.

    After experiencing the wonderful world of loans ask yourself:

    Was it worth it?

    How much more than the actual cost of the item did I end up paying ?

    Which is the best option, loans or saving?

How To Borrow Wisely

Despite the dangers of borrowing, there *are* times when a loan may be necessary. Some people find themselves in an emergency situation: they need a loan to get a place to live, or to pay for an operation, or to help a loved one in need.

Sometimes borrowing money is actually a wise financial move. If a loan enables you to make an *appreciating investment* (one that goes up in value) the money you make can offset the cost of the interest. For example, as you get older you might consider borrowing money to purchase a computer and printer if you're confident in your ability to make money as a writer or graphic artist.

Many people borrow money to buy a house, figuring that it's better to invest their rent money in something they can sell someday. And if real estate prices go up, they may make money even after accounting for the interest they paid on the loan.

Debt Victory

Talk to adults who have had some trouble with getting into debt. Find out how they won the debt victory. Ask any other questions you think are relevant or helpful to get an idea of the cost of borrowing.

    1. How did they get out of debt?

    2. What was the affect on them and their families?

    3. What did it end up costing them?

    4. Would they do it again?

Make a list of what you think are the benefits of borrowing and what are the downfalls. Which list is longer?

Benefits:

1. _____

2. _____

3. _____

4. _____

5. _____

Downfalls:

1. _____

2. _____

3. _____

4. _____

5. _____

Rewind

1. Borrowing is expensive. Instead of earning interest, you're paying it.

2. Borrowing is habit-forming. When a chunk of your money has to pay off things you bought in the past, there's less money to pay cash for what you need now. So then you borrow more.

3. Borrowing is destructive. It can destroy your finances, credit, and put big strains on your family and friendships.

4. Borrowing money for a house, education, or business can help you *if* the investment appreciates more than the cost of the loan.

CHAPTER
How To Change the World with Your Money

Chapter 12

How To Change the World with Your Money

Lots of teenagers say that they're not old enough, smart enough, or rich enough to change the world. So they sit around and wait for that magical age when God can finally use them to make a difference. Guess what? God doesn't check for IDs at the kingdom door. He can use you right now to have a big effect on your community and culture. So, get out your money and use it to change the world.

Vote with Your Money

Every dollar you spend on something is a vote for the values that product conveys. Every time you pay $7 to watch a violent film, you're saying to Hollywood: "Violence sells; make more violent films."

When you buy a CD, cassette, or video that celebrates the Christian faith, you are telling the musicians, the record companies, and the movie producers to make more Christian products. Every purchase is a vote. When you buy *good* stuff, you're voting for *more* good stuff.

Lots of folks complain about the bad language and violence they see in movies, music, TV, video games, books, and magazines. Then they vote *for* these things by buying them. Most of the people who produce these things aren't dead set on making the world a trashier place. They're just trying to make money, and if the bad stuff sells, they'll continue to make it. If they could make more money producing good stuff, they'd make more good stuff. And those who are already making good stuff would make a lot more of it.

You might be saying, "I'm just one vote. They won't notice *what* I do." You're right. Your purchase alone isn't going to make or break them. But it still counts. When your friends decide to go to a trashy movie, you could politely excuse yourself. When they ask why, tell them. Of course, some will laugh at you, and they'll probably go anyway—without you. But maybe your best friend won't go. That's two votes!

And if you can convince them to see a better movie, maybe that's three or four votes. When you do this several times, with enough friends, and enough of *their* friends, people start to talk. Then it becomes an *issue*, and that makes a difference. If enough people go to good movies instead of bad ones, the theater notices.

Even if your "votes" have no effect on the producers of the world's products, when you buy bad things, you're contributing to what's bad. When you buy good things, you're contributing to what's good. It's important to live and act according to your beliefs. Vote with your money as your conscience tells you to.

There's one more reason to vote with your money. It's God's money! Remember, you're just managing it for Him. And He does care what you do with it. Use His money well, for *good* things.

Be a Consumer Watchdog

Scan newspapers or magazines for a couple of weeks.

1. Find consumer-related articles that you may have questions about and that would effect your purchasing decisions and cut them out.

2. Follow the stories for a couple of weeks. Keep the relevant articles. If it turns out to be a problem with products or with what the companies are doing, take the articles and photocopy them. Show your investigation to your friends, parents, or even your teacher.

Shop Locally

Some people are funny. They'll drive around a parking lot for ten minutes just to get the closest parking space. They'll risk life and limb, racing and weaving through traffic, just so they can get home one minute faster. They'll burn two dollars in gasoline to drive across town so they can save a buck at a cheaper gas station. But *first, fastest, cheapest* isn't always *best*.

This is especially true with money. Let's say that you're shopping for shoes. You've got your heart set on a new pair of state-of-the-art sneakers: They've got hydro-electric soles, titanium-alloy heal supports, and remote-control laces. Your neighborhood shoe store sells them for $65. The big discount store in the next town sells them for $55. Why waste $10? So you hop in the car, drive an hour round-trip, and get the ultimate shoes for the ultimate price. And if price is most important, you will have made the right move. But look at the big picture.

DISCOUNT-O-RAMA	
shoes	$ 55
gas to drive there	4
impulse CD purchase	10
1 hour of mom's time	?
air pollution	?
income lost to local citizens	65
taxes lost to community	?
Total cost	$69

(plus impact on family, environment, community, and taxes)

DIPPY'S SHOE STORE	
shoes	$65
(walk to store)	0
(no CDs at Dippy's)	0
(don't need driver)	0
(clean air commute)	0
(no loss to local store)	0
(no loss to local taxes)	0
Total cost	$65

First of all, you spent $4 in gas. Okay, so you saved *$6*. But while you were at the discount store, you spotted a "great price" on CDs (they sell *everything* there), so you picked one up for $10. Now you've actually spent *more* money because you had no intention of buying that CD (and you may be sick of listening to it in a week anyway).

There are other "prices" too. There's the extra air pollution from driving all those miles—not to mention the one hour your mom had to sacrifice away from home to be your chauffeur. There's also a community price. The owner of your local shoe store lives in your town, employs your neighbors, sends his or her kids to your school, and pays taxes that pay for your police, fire department, street repair, and the upkeep of that park where you hang out.

When you spend your money locally, you invest in your community. And when you *vote with your money* in your community, you have a powerful effect on lives.

Does this mean it's wrong to shop outside your community? Of course not. But it *does* mean that, as God's manager, it's wise to look at *all* the price tags: financial, social, spiritual. Make every one of God's dollars do the most *good* to honor Him.

Invest Locally

There's another way to be sure that your money makes a difference in your community. Deposit it in a local bank. It's easy to understand why a neighborhood store is an important part of the community. People have to eat. But why is a local bank important?

It goes like this: The bank uses the money in your savings account to make loans to people and businesses in your community. Let's say that the bank took that money, combined it with lots of other accounts, and lent it to a woman to help her open a sporting goods store. She used the money to pay a carpenter to renovate the building.

The carpenter used some of the money to buy lumber. The lumberyard owner used some of *that* money to hire a new manager. The manager used some of his new salary to pay the property taxes on his house. The schools used some of the property taxes to buy computers for their classrooms. The students who use these computers will become more successful. They'll earn more money, deposit more of it at the bank, and the bank will lend more money to other businesses . . . and so on.

And we didn't even mention the employees that were hired at the new sporting goods store, and where they spent *their* paychecks. Nor did we mention how much money some of these people gave back to God, and what they voted on with their money, and . . . you get the picture.

When possible, *invest* in your community.

Check Out the Big League Corporations

Look at Coca Cola, McDonalds, or others. Write a letter to the companies, or e-mail or visit their Web sites. Ask them for a copy of their code of ethics or core values. What do they feel is their business' ethical backbone?

Give, Give, Give

We talked about giving in another chapter. Giving is the most powerful way to change the world with your money. God always does good things with "your" money when you give it wisely.

The world is filled to the brim with great needs. And governments can argue till the end of time about how to solve these problems. But you can do something *now*.

Every month that you give makes you a world changer. You are part of the solution. And God applauds your efforts because you're showing that your priorities are His priorities. Make an impact on the world with *His* money—used the way it should be.

Rewind

1. Every time you buy something, you are *voting* with your money. Buy *good* things, and the people who make them will make more.

2. Buying locally supports the people and services in your own community. And it gives you a bigger vote in what's best for your community.

3. Investing locally puts your money to work in the lives of your neighbors.

4. Regular giving makes you a part of the solution to the world's problems.

notes

_____

_____

_____

_____

_____

_____

_____

_____

_____

_____

notes

Blank Checks

CATEGORY# _____   CHECK # _____

                                          DATE _____

PAY TO THE
ORDER OF _____ $ _____

_____DOLLARS

BANK OF _____

                                          _____

CATEGORY# _____   CHECK # _____

                                          DATE _____

PAY TO THE
ORDER OF _____ $ _____

_____DOLLARS

BANK OF _____

                                          _____

CATEGORY# _____   CHECK # _____

                                          DATE _____

PAY TO THE
ORDER OF _____ $ _____

_____DOLLARS

BANK OF _____

                                          _____

Check Register

DATE	TRANSACTION	DEPOSIT (+)		WITHDRAWAL (-)		BALANCE	

DATE	TRANSACTION	DEPOSIT (+)		WITHDRAWAL (-)		BALANCE	

Withdrawal Slips

Date	Initials	Account No.		WITHDRAW
Amount in Words			Amount $	
Name (Please Print)		Please sign in teller's presence		
		Signature - Cash Received		

Date	Initials	Account No.		WITHDRAW
Amount in Words			Amount $	
Name (Please Print)		Please sign in teller's presence		
		Signature - Cash Received		

Deposit Slips

		Cash	x5		**Checks**	DEPOSIT
Date	Initials		x10			
			x20			
			x50			
Please sign in teller's presence			x100			
Signature - Cash Received			Coin			
			Total $		**Subtotal**	
					Less Cash Received	
Account No.		Name (Please Print)			Amount $	

		Cash	x5		**Checks**	DEPOSIT
Date	Initials		x10			
			x20			
			x50			
Please sign in teller's presence			x100			
Signature - Cash Received			Coin			
			Total $		**Subtotal**	
					Less Cash Received	
Account No.		Name (Please Print)			Amount $	

Individual Account Sheets

ACCOUNT NAME

DATE	TRANSACTION	DEPOSIT	W/DRAW	BALANCE

Monthly Income & Expenses

Annual Income _____

Monthly Income _____

LESS

1. Charitable Giving _____
2. Tax _____

NET SPENDABLE INCOME _____

3. **Housing (30%)** _____
   - Mortgage (Rent) _____
   - Insurance _____
   - Taxes _____
   - Electricity _____
   - Gas _____
   - Water _____
   - Sanitation _____
   - Telephone _____
   - Maintenance _____
   - Other _____

4. **Food (17%)** _____

5. **Auto(s) (15%)** _____
   - Payments _____
   - Gas & Oil _____
   - Insurance _____
   - License _____
   - Taxes _____
   - Maint/Repair/
     Replacement _____

6. **Insurance (5%)** _____
   - Life _____
   - Medical _____
   - Other _____

7. **Debts (5%)** _____
   - Credit Cards _____
   - Loans & Notes _____
   - Other _____

8. **Enter. / Recreation (7%)** _____
   - Eating Out _____
   - Trips _____
   - Babysitters _____
   - Activities _____
   - Vacation _____
   - Other _____

9. **Clothing (5%)** _____

10. **Savings (5%)** _____

11. **Medical Expenses (5%)** _____
    - Doctor _____
    - Dental _____
    - Drugs _____
    - Other _____

12. **Miscellaneous (6%)** _____
    - Toiletry, Cosmetics _____
    - Beauty, Barber _____
    - Laundry, Cleaning _____
    - Allowances, Lunches _____
    - Subscriptions, Gifts _____
      (Incl. Christmas)
    - Special Education _____
    - Cash _____
    - Other _____

TOTAL EXPENSES _____

Net Spendable Income _____

Difference _____

Christian Financial Concepts

Teaching | Biblical Principles of Managing Money

Larry Burkett, founder and president of Christian Financial Concepts, is the best-selling author of more than 50 books on business and personal finances. He also hosts two of CFC's four radio programs broadcast on hundreds of stations worldwide.

Larry earned B.S. degrees in marketing and in finance, and recently an Honorary Doctorate in Economics was conferred by Southwest Baptist University. For several years Larry served as manager in the space program at Cape Canaveral, Florida. He also has been vice president of an electronics manufacturing firm. Larry's education, business experience, and solid understanding of God's Word enable him to give practical, Bible-based financial counsel to families, churches, and businesses.

Founded in 1976, Christian Financial Concepts is a nonprofit, nondenominational ministry dedicated to helping God's people gain a clear understanding of how to manage their money according to scriptural principles. Although practical assistance is provided on many levels, the purpose of CFC is simply *to bring glory to God by freeing His people from financial bondage so they may serve Him to their utmost.*

One major avenue of ministry involves the training of volunteers in budget and debt counseling and linking them with financially troubled families and individuals through a nationwide referral network. CFC also provides financial management seminars and workshops for church and other groups. (Formats available include audio, video, and live instruction.) A full line of printed and audio-visual materials related to money management is available through CFC's materials department (1–800–722–1976) or via the Internet (http://www.cfcministry.org).

Life Pathways, another outreach of Christian Financial Concepts, helps teenagers and adults find their occupational calling. The Life Pathways *Career Direct* assessment package gauges a person's work priorities, skills, vocational interests, and personality. Reports in each of these areas define a person's strengths, weaknesses, and unique, God-given pattern for work.

Visit CFC's Internet site at http://www.cfcministry.org or write to the address below for further information.

Christian Financial Concepts
PO Box 2377
Gainesville, GA 30503

Money Matters for Kids and Teens™
Teaching Kids to Manage God's Gifts

Lauree and L. Allen Burkett are the founders of **Money Matters for Kids™**. God has planted in their hearts the commitment to see the next generation grounded in God's Word and living His principles. The vision of **Money Matters for Kids™** is to provide children and teens with the tools they need to understand the biblical principles of stewardship and to encourage them to live by those principles.

Visit our Web site at: **www.mmforkids.org.** We welcome your comments and suggestions.

Money Matters for Kids
Lynden, Washington 98264–9760

building Christian faith in families

Lightwave Publishing is a recognized leader in developing quality resources that encourage, assist, and equip parents to build Christian faith in their families.

Lightwave Publishing also has a fun kids' Web site and an Internet-based newsletter called *Tips & Tools for Spiritual Parenting*. This newsletter helps parents with issues such as answering their children's questions, helping make church more exciting, teaching children how to pray, and much more.

For more information, visit Lightwave's Web site at: **www.lightwavepublishing.com**

Moody Press, a ministry of Moody Bible Institute, is designed for education, evangelization, and edification.

If we may assist you in knowing more about Christ and the Christian life, please write us without obligation:

Moody Press, c/o MLM
Chicago, Illinois 60610

Or visit us at Moody's Web site: **www.moodypress.org**